The 3 Keys to Empowerment

Release the Power within People for Astonishing Results

Ken Blanchard
John P. Carlos
Alan Randolph

EasyRead Large

Copyright Page from the Original Book

The 3 Keys to Empowerment

 Berrett-Koehler Publishers, Inc.
235 Montgomery Street, Suite 650
San Francisco, California 94104-2916
Tel: (415) 288-0260, Fax: (415) 362-2512
www.bkconnection.com

Ordering information for print editions
Quantity sales. Special discounts are available on quantity purchases by corporations, associations, and others. For details, contact the "Special Sales Department" at the Berrett-Koehler address above.
Individual sales. Berrett-Koehler publications are available through most bookstores. They can also be ordered directly from Berrett-Koehler: Tel: (800) 929-2929; Fax: (802) 864-7626; www.bkconnection.com
Orders for college textbook/course adoption use. Please contact Berrett-Koehler: Tel: (800) 929-2929; Fax: (802) 864-7626.
Orders by U.S. trade bookstores and wholesalers. Please contact Ingram Publisher Services, Tel: (800) 509-4887; Fax: (800) 838-1149; E-mail: customer.service@ingrampublisherservices.com; or visit www.ingram publisherservices.com/Ordering for details about electronic ordering.

Berrett-Koehler and the BK logo are registered trademarks of Berrett-Koehler Publishers, Inc.

First Edition
Hardcover print edition ISBN 978-1-57675-060-5
Paperback print edition ISBN 978-1-57675-160-2
PDF e-book ISBN 978-1-60509-340-6

2009-1

Proofreading: PeopleSpeak
Interior design and production: Joel Friedlander, Marin Bookworks
Indexing: Leonard Rosenbaum
Cover design: Richard Adelson

TABLE OF CONTENTS

Dedicated
To all the pioneers of empowerment,
the leaders, teams, and organizations
who have taught us so much!

To Margie McKee Blanchard
My cofounder, coauthor, friend, and inspirational
partner!

To C. Lynne Carlos
My partner, friend, and wife for thirty-two years and
counting!

To Ruth Anne Gray Randolph My best friend and
partner in life!

Preface

Our first book on empowerment, titled *Empowerment Takes More Than a Minute* and published in 1996 by Berrett-Koehler Publishers, has been a popular introduction to the challenges of creating a culture of empowerment. We have been gratified to see it on the *Business Week* Best Sellers List and to have it translated into ten languages besides English. By all accounts this book has been a success and has helped many managers and employees *release the power within people for astonishing results.*

What has been apparent also is that efforts to move to empowerment always raise questions for managers and employees alike. These questions are often quite detailed, and their answers were not always apparent in our first book. This second book, *The 3 Keys to Empowerment,* asks and answers those questions and provides a three-stage road map for the journey of changing to empowerment.

Everyone seems to agree that employees, managers, and companies can benefit from creating a culture in which people could be empowered. Involving employees in an empowered culture allows them to use their knowledge, experience, and internal motivation to accomplish tasks for the organization. Employees become team members who are accountable for results that benefit the organization in both tangible and intangible ways. Employees also experience a sense of ownership, excitement, and pride in their work. Managers become team leaders who facilitate the involvement of team members. They find that results are achieved much easier than in a hierarchical culture, and they develop a new sense of pride from developing empowered teams that achieve far more than anyone thought possible.

The difficulty that everyone experiences is that talking about empowerment is a lot easier than creating a culture in which it can prosper. The title of our first book was designed to let people know that the movement from hierarchy to empowerment would not be easy. It would take more than an announcement, more than a wish, more than a small effort, indeed, "more than a minute." It is not an easy task to give up the assumptions, behaviors, and systems (policies and procedures) that worked well in a hierarchical culture and replace them with assumptions, behaviors, and systems that support and expect empowerment, but it is doable in steps and in stages.

The 3 Keys to Empowerment is intended to be a guidebook for the journey. It is not a book designed for you to sit down and read in a few sittings, except to gain an overview of the issues. Rather, it is a user's guide for the journey to Empowerment. *The 3 Keys to Empowerment* will help you keep on task and will definitely increase the speed of your journey. Think of your questions as you progress, find them in the various sections, and also find your answers. We know that this guidebook will make your journey much easier and will give you the confidence to continue.

If you have questions that you cannot find in this book, please send them to us and we will provide you with our best thinking on that issue. We want you to succeed in reaching empowerment, so let this guidebook—and us as references—help you along the way.

Good luck to you as you undertake this most important and challenging journey! We are confident that the effort is worth it because in empowerment, you will *release the power within people for astonishing results.*

Ken Blanchard John Carlos Alan Randolph

INTRODUCTION

THE CHALLENGE OF MOVING TO EMPOWERMENT

Empowerment has been and remains one of the most promising but least understood concepts in business to date. First introduced in the 1980s, it quickly became a buzzword full of promise but short on delivery. Who could argue with the end result of empowerment? Ask senior managers if they want employees who accept responsibility, have a proprietary interest in the company, and want to work hard for company results, and the answer is, of course, yes. Ask employees if they want to feel valued, be involved in their jobs, and feel pride in the work they do, and the answer is, of course, yes.

Essentially, managers and employees want the same outcome. So why has it been so hard to achieve empowerment? Why has the concept fallen into disrepute? The answer is both simple and complex.

First, it is not the concept of empowerment that is flawed. Rather, it is people's lack of understanding of how to move from a more traditional hierarchical mind-set to a mind-set of empowerment.

Too many managers view empowerment as giving people the power to make decisions. And too many employees view empowerment as being given free rein to do what they want to do. What we offer in this section is a better understanding of what empowerment really is—a releasing of the power within people to achieve astonishing results. What we also offer is a macro-level understanding of the process and issues that must be addressed to create a culture of empowerment.

CHAPTER 1

Releasing the Power within People

Empowerment. Can it work for you, or is it just another buzzword for the ages? We believe that empowerment (which we link with team member involvement, ownership, responsibility, proprietary interest, and pride) is crucial for companies to be competitive in today's business world and certainly in the world of tomorrow. Literally, for companies to succeed in the new world of business, team members must feel that they own their jobs and that they have key roles. And many of the most successful and admired companies in the world agree.

WHY MAKE THE EFFORT TO CHANGE TO EMPOWERMENT?

A variety of external challenges have paved the way for forces of change to bombard people and their organizations from all sides. First, customers have developed very high expectations regarding quality, price, and service. The feeling is that if your company cannot meet their needs, they will find another company that can. Second, these pressures from customers must be managed in light of the need to remain profitable. There is always the danger of providing what the customer wants while under-cutting margins to the point of risking company viability. Third, the forces of change brought on by global competition, new technologies, and customer mind shifts mean that whatever was outstanding last year may be ordinary this year. The bar is continually being raised, and unless your company and its people can jump over it, a competitor will gladly take your place. Fourth, the members of today's work force are quite different from those of the past. They have a tremendous potential for growth and development but an impatience for controlling their own destinies. There is an ongoing need to create greater trust between team members and leaders so that people can and will put forth their best efforts to act with responsibility in a context of freedom and so that leaders can and will allow their team members to act with responsibility and freedom.

Creating a culture of empowerment is not easy—it means acting with strength in the face of adversity while living with a delicate balance of responsibility and freedom. But once you start down this path to empowerment, there really is no turning back, unless you wish the forces of change to overwhelm you and everyone else in the organization. To make matters even more challenging, the compelling internal forces for change leave leaders and team members with no choice but to consider empowerment.

As we have worked with clients over the last few years, we have learned that the old deal between companies and their employees has changed. No longer does loyalty guarantee job security. During the 1950s, if someone took a job with a Fortune 500 company he or she was "set for life." Is this true now? Of course not! Some of the biggest layoffs have occurred at some of the biggest companies. But layoffs do not guarantee company success. So what is the new deal?

When asked what they want from people today, leaders almost universally respond, "We want people who are problem solvers, who take initiative, and who act like they own the business." What they are saying is that they want empowered people. But what about the team members; what do they want in the new deal? When we ask these people, they respond, "We want honesty. Tell us the truth about how our company is doing; we can handle it and we can help improve the situation. In addition, we want to learn new skills that will not only help us here but we can take with us if we have to look for another job." What they are saying is that they want a new deal for involvement. *They want to be empowered.*

WHAT IS EMPOWERMENT?

In many ways then, leaders and team members want the same thing—empowerment. Indeed, empowerment is a cutting-edge "technology" that provides both the strategic advantage companies are seeking and the opportunity people are seeking. It is the means for involving team members as business partners in determining company success or failure (which today is defined as being simultaneously customer driven, cost effective, fast and flexible, and continuously improving).

Empowerment can assist any leader (who is willing to make some key changes) tap the knowledge, skills, experience, and motivation of every person in the company. Leaders who empower people are placing additional responsibility for results on the team members. That is right: *empowerment is not soft management.* But even though it places high expectations on people, team members embrace empowerment because it leads to the joys of involvement, ownership, and growth. Unfortunately, too few leaders and team members understand how to create a culture of empowerment.

While giving people the authority and responsibility to make important business decisions is a key structural aspect of empowerment, it is not the whole picture, as some leaders mistakenly think. *The real essence of empowerment comes from releasing the knowledge, experience, and motivational power that is already in people but is being severely underutilized.* In hierarchical organizations using more traditional "command and control" management practices, the organization's human resource capacity is only partially tapped, perhaps at 25 to 30 percent of capacity. And we all know what would happen if equipment was utilized at only 25 to 30 percent of capacity. The company would suffer greatly and management might have a short career, indeed. Why should we accept the same low capacity utilization from people? Empowerment can help every leader increase the performance capacity of people in any organization.

DOES EMPOWERMENT REALLY WORK?

A valid question to ask is, Does empowerment really work? In an era when competition is fierce, any company that cannot produce at a lower cost, with better quality, and at a faster pace than its global competitors may soon be out of business. At the level of team members, the result will be loss of jobs, with more work piled on those who are left behind. Leaders will feel the stress of producing more with fewer people and with a wider span of control. It is for these very reasons that the traditional management model of "the manager in control and the employees being controlled" does not work. What every leader is seeking is solutions to make his or her job—achieving results with fewer re-sources—easier. At the same time, team members are searching for job security, ownership, and a renewed sense of pride in their work. We believe firmly that empowerment is a significant part of the solution to these issues.

In the book *Employee Involvement and Total Quality Management,* Ed Lawler and his colleagues in the Center for Organizational Effectiveness at the University of Southern California support this conclusion.[1] They report that when people are given more control and responsibility over their jobs, companies achieve a greater return on sales (10.3 percent) than those companies that do not involve people (6.3 percent). One of our clients in the mature retail food industry found that annual sales growth increased from 15 percent to 26 percent; sales per store increased 10 percent per year, while the number of stores increased almost 100 percent and overall sales volume increased in excess of 500 percent over eight years. Another client in the engineering services industry has used better information sharing and a team approach (two of the keys to empowerment) to reduce project execution costs by 40 percent, while maintaining high quality work. Indeed, empowerment works for those leaders and companies that make the effort to change.

A convenience store chain on the West Coast has used empowerment practices to reduce turnover from the industry average range of 140 to 220 percent per year to 70 percent per year—not as good as other industries but still quite a cost saver. And management has learned that fewer people leave the company unhappy. A typical response from a former convenience store team member is "I was told to sell my soul for a minimum-wage job." When people leave this company, their response is more likely to be, "As an eighteen year old, I had probably the best first job experience I could imagine. I plan to be a customer of theirs for a long time to come." What's the bottom line? The company may lose people faster than they like, but it may be gaining customers for the long run!

HOW HARD IS IT TO MOVE TO EMPOWERMENT?

Far more companies talk about empowerment than practice it. Too many leaders think that if they and their people want empowerment, it will "just happen naturally." Nothing could be further from the truth. The change is too fundamental and involves replacing many old habits with new habits. To change to empowerment takes an understanding of what empowerment really is, knowledge of key action steps, and a dedicated effort. According to Lawler and his colleagues, even companies that use empowerment programs involve less than 20 percent of their workforce. And our experience suggests that many companies start an empowerment effort only to stop the journey somewhere during the process of change, thus feeding the belief that empowerment is just another "flavor of the month." Indeed, empowerment is not as easy to create as it first appears.

The main reason empowerment is "easier said than done" is that managers often think that all they have to do to empower people is to "give team members the authority to make decisions or to mandate a change in behavior." By so doing, leaders believe they are giving people the freedom to act. At the same time, they often perceive a reluctance by team members to be held accountable for decisions they make. Team members say they want control over decisions and involvement, but they think that leaders add constraints that inhibit their taking responsibility. The vast majority of leaders unintentionally do not provide an adequate mix of knowledge, information, power, and rewards to create a culture in which people can become empowered. Nor do they change the way in which team members' performance is measured. And people are not automatically prepared to take on the challenges of being empowered. They often think they want to be empowered until they learn what it really means in terms of the changes they as team members must make.

The source of these difficulties lies in the tremendous shift in thinking that is needed by both leaders and team members. Empowerment challenges many of the most basic assumptions about organizations that leaders and team members have come to accept as fact. The kind of thinking that led to individual and corporate success in the past is no longer valid in the world of empowerment. Attitudes, behaviors, practices, and ways of relating must change for an organization and its team members and leaders to become empowered.

WHAT ARE THE KEY CONCEPTS FOR NAVIGATING THE JOURNEY TO EMPOWERMENT?

This book will provide in-depth descriptions of the actions that have to be taken to successfully navigate the difficult journey to empowerment. To do so we will integrate three sets of concepts:

- The three keys to creating empowerment in an organization that we discussed in *Empowerment Takes More Than a Minute.*
- The three stages of the process of changing to empowerment through which every leader and team member must travel to achieve empowerment.

- Situational Leadership® II, a framework that has proven valuable for leaders, whether they are working one-on-one with people, in teams, or at the organizational level (department, division, or the total organization) and for team members in their self-leadership efforts.

THE THREE KEYS TO EMPOWERMENT (FROM EMPOWERMENT TAKES MORE THAN A MINUTE)[2]

KEY #1: SHARE INFORMATION WITH EVERYONE

The first (and often misunderstood) key to empowerment is *information sharing.* As a leader, you do not, surprisingly, start the journey by sharing your vision of empowerment. Rather, you start by sharing whatever information you have about your business with your people. We have learned from our clients and research that without information to understand the business and its needs, team members will see empowerment as just another management idea. They will not trust that change will really occur, and perhaps rightly so. When leaders are willing to share whatever information they have—both good and bad—they begin to gain the trust of their people, who then feel included and trusted by leadership. Furthermore, it should be obvious (though it does not appear to be understood by many leaders) that people without information cannot possibly act responsibly. They cannot be expected to make good business decisions without the same information their leaders have used to make those kinds of decisions in the past. On the other hand, with information, people are almost compelled to act with responsibility. Information sharing gives the empowerment process a kick start that is essential to a successful journey.

KEY #2: CREATE AUTONOMY THROUGH BOUNDARIES

Paradoxically, while empowerment involves minimizing structure so people can operate autonomously, leaders must begin the process of changing to empowerment by imposing more, rather than less, structure. Working in conjunction with information sharing, the second key to empowerment clarifies the need to create autonomy by establishing boundaries. To be sure, the kind of structure we mean is not the same as that found in traditional hierarchies. In a hierarchy, structure is created to inhibit the behavior of people. Rules, procedures, policies, and management reporting relationships are all designed to inform people about what they cannot do or how they must do a task. In empowerment, the structures have a different purpose and take different forms. Now the structure is intended to inform team members about the ranges within which they can act with autonomy. For example, the boundaries in a culture of empowerment take the form of vision statements, collaborative goals, decision-making rules, and performance management partnerships. Within the ranges set by those boundaries, team members can determine what to do and how to do it. As the empowerment process unfolds, the range of structures can widen and deepen to allow people greater degrees of control and responsibility.

KEY #3: TEAMS BECOME THE HIERARCHY

The third vital key that must work in harmony with the other two is gradually replacing the old hierarchy's purpose and functions with self-directed teams. Many of today's complex business decisions require input from a collection of people if those decisions are to be effective. And implementation of the decisions requires team effort if they are to have the desired results. *The bottom line is that teams are more effective than individuals in complex situations.* The team—with its synergy of effort—offers greater knowledge, plus a support mechanism for people who are trying to act in an empowered fashion. But empowered, self-directed teams are quite different from participative teams, quality circles, or semi-autonomous teams. They make and implement decisions and are held accountable for results; they do not just recommend ideas. Because they are so different, self-directed teams must be developed over time, and team leaders must learn how to work with and in these high performing teams.

THE THREE STAGES IN THE PROCESS OF CHANGING TO EMPOWERMENT

The journey to empowerment is full of challenges, and it requires dedication to see it through to the finish. As with any change that involves habits, attitudes, and behaviors of both leaders and team members, coupled with systems and organizational changes, the journey will involve many ups and downs along the way. In fact, there are three stages of the change process that are clearly distinguishable and that involve different issues, feelings, and needs.

STAGE 1: STARTING AND ORIENTING THE JOURNEY

This first stage of the process of changing to empowerment involves beginning to act and commit to change. It is a time when people throughout the organization will have mixed feelings. On the one hand, team members and leaders will wonder where this journey is actually going to take them and why there is such a strong need to change the way the company is now. On the other hand, they will like the idea of becoming more involved in their work lives and using their many talents each day at work. But there is a naivete that people have at this stage of the change process. On the surface, the idea of empowerment is appealing to both leaders and team members, but underneath there is a feeling of concern over venturing into the unknown world of empowerment, as well as doubt about senior management's sincerity about changing to empowerment.

STAGE 2: CHANGE AND DISCOURAGEMENT

Somewhere along the journey, people will gain enough knowledge about where they are headed to realize that they are not sure how to get there. It may be a few months into the process of changing to empowerment before this feeling of uncertainty sur-faces, but it will inevitably come into focus at some time. When it does occur, people are going to feel a sense of discouragement and frustration. They will probably wonder why the change to empowerment was ever started. Leaders may fear that team members will never rise to the challenge and responsibility of being empowered. At the same time, team members will experience a growing doubt that leadership will stay the course to empowerment. The essence is that leaders and team members will feel disillusioned and in need of some strong leadership that is capable of providing guidance and encouragement. Unfortu-nately, if we look to the top of the organization, senior leadership will likely be experiencing some of these same feelings of discouragement as these executives wonder what they have created, how long empower-ment will take, and what to do next. The result is of-ten a true "leadership vacuum" that strikes fear and doubt into the hearts and minds of all parties involved. It is at this juncture that many organizations, teams, and leaders give up on the journey. This is unfortunate because this valley of discouragement is natural and is also the doorway leading to empowerment.

STAGE 3: ADOPTING AND REFINING EMPOWERMENT

Those who stay the course will see people in an organization (leaders, team members, and senior leadership) begin to adopt the new habits, attitudes, and behaviors of empowerment and will sense that light is really coming through the tunnel. The newly developing habits, though, will not yet have solidified to the point where they feel natural. People will be acting with greater responsibility as partners with leaders in a team environment. And leaders will be more comfortable with the idea of sharing responsibility and control with people as team members. The challenge for all involved is to keep moving ahead toward full empowerment without becoming complacent about accomplishments to date. Most members of the organization will be on board with the new culture, though still learning it. A few others will be lagging back, needing support, encouragement, and clear expectations to get up to speed. It is a time for refinement and for feeling satisfaction about how far everyone has come on the journey. But the journey is not yet complete, and leaders and team members know it. The difference now is that the finish line is in sight, and most people understand the vision of the new culture and are working hard to achieve it.

SITUATIONAL LEADERSHIP® II

Reaching empowerment involves a strong commitment to the end goal, but it also involves effective leadership and a plan of action. As a starting point, it is helpful to think of leadership as an influence process. Any time you try to influence the behavior of someone else to accomplish the goals of an organization, you are engaging in an act of leadership. In the context of moving to empowerment, leadership is vital, according to our colleague Drea Zigarmi, in four domains or contexts.

The first context is the self-leadership domain. One goal of empowerment is that people will eventually become self-reliant achievers. Rather than waiting to be told what to do, they will anticipate what needs to be done and take appropriate action on their own. The second context is the one-on-one domain. Here a leader tries to influence someone else whether the person is a direct report, peer or associate, a boss, or even a customer. The third context is the team domain. Today, more and more leaders find that they need to influence people in teams or small groups of three to twelve people. Indeed, the team members must learn to influence each other if the team is to be effective. The fourth and final context in which leadership takes place is the organizational domain. Here the leader heads up the entire organization or leads a large subunit—such as a division or major functional area like marketing—within an organization. While the leader may have a group of direct reports with whom he or she teams, these direct reports have people who report to them. In this domain, leaders influence more than one level below them in the organizational structure.

To create a culture of empowerment, people must behave in different ways than would commonly occur in a hierarchical culture. In many ways, this change of behavior involves a movement from dependence on the leadership of others to independence from, or interdependence with, external leadership. This requires a shift in the traditional leadership paradigm. Rather than seeing leaders as directing, controlling, and supervising the behavior of others or even supporting, encouraging, and facilitating their efforts, the desired situation is one where the necessary direction and support come from individual and team initiatives. A helpful framework for understanding and guiding this journey is Situational Leadership® II.[3]

Situational Leadership® II was first developed for the one-on-one leadership domain. Later its application to the three other leadership domains was discovered. To help you understand the richness of this simple but powerful model and how useful it will be in guiding the journey from hierarchy to empowerment, the next chapter will be completely devoted to an explanation of how it applies across all four leadership domains (self, one-on-one, team, and organization).

THE PLAN FOR THIS BOOK

The plan for this book is to focus on how to use the three keys to empowerment within each of the three stages of change, with Situational Leadership® II (as explained in chapter 2) as an overarching framework. We realize that each organization and its people will encounter their own unique situations and sets of dynamics. By addressing each of the three keys as they should operate in each of the three stages of the change process, leaders will be able to develop a unique action plan that will get results. Hence, we will devote nine chapters (chapters 3-11) to this exploration. The general format will be to ask and answer questions that we have heard from leaders and team members that relate to each key within each stage of change. We hope that we will address your questions in a way that is meaningful to you. *As you read through the book, you may notice that some of the action items that respond to the questions are similar, if not the same, from stage to stage and even from key to key. The reason is that some issues persist; they need repeated focus if change is to occur.*

We recommend that you read through the book to get an overview of the issues that will arise at each stage of the change process. Then use the book as an action guide by focusing on each stage of change as it occurs for you and the actions that will help you deal with the relevant issues. For example, if you are just beginning, go to the three chapters in the section on "Starting and Orienting the Journey" (chapters 3-5). If you are already in the stage of discouragement, jump to the three chapters in the section on "Change and Discouragement" (chapters 6-8). And if you have been working toward empowerment for a while and feel it is within sight, go to the final section on "Adopting and Refining Empowerment" (chapters 9-11). From wherever you are, use the appropriate chapters to answer your key questions and provide guidance for your action plan. And use the matrix in chapter 12 as a synopsis that will help you keep the big picture and the interconnection of actions in mind.

Reaching empowerment is a challenging journey that requires persistence and a plan for action. It also requires thoughtful reflection in concert with action. We are confident that *The 3 Keys to Empowerment* will provide you with the detailed game plan that will allow you and those around you in your organization to realize the many powerful and satisfying benefits of creating a culture of empowerment. Let's get started on that challenging but rewarding journey by teaching you in chapter 2 all about Situational Leadership® II as an overall framework for understanding and guiding the journey.

CHAPTER 2

Using Situational Leadership® II to Guide the Journey

Situational Leadership® II is a powerful, yet simple, contingency-based model of how to alter leadership approaches to fit various situations. In this chapter we will explore how this model can be useful as a framework for guiding the journey to empowerment. As a starting point, let us look first at the various concerns people will have as they make the change to empowerment. As we discussed in the previous chapter, there are three stages along the journey—(1) Starting and Orienting the Journey, (2) Change and Discouragement, and (3) Adopting and Refining Empowerment. As people pass through each of these stages of change, a variety of concerns must be recognized and addressed if the destination of empowerment is to be reached.

A U.S. Department of Education research project at the University of Texas identified six predictable and sequential concerns that people experience in making a significant change.[1] During the initial stage of Starting and Orienting the Journey, people will express and want answers to *information concerns* and *personal concerns.* As they move into the second stage of Change and Discouragement, they will express and want answers to *implementation concerns* and *impact concerns.* Finally, in the last stage of Adopting and Refining Empowerment, they will express concerns that suggest the destination is in sight, namely, *collaboration concerns* and *refinement concerns.* If these six concerns are addressed, the destination of empowerment can be reached. If they are not addressed, the journey will surely bog down or, worse yet, end in disaster. Let us explain these concerns in more detail and then look at how Situational Leadership® II provides a framework for addressing them.

Essentially, the concerns are expressed as a variety of questions. Consider the following:

1. *Information Concerns*—What is the change? Why is it needed? What is wrong with the way things are now? People with information concerns don't want to be *sold* on the change; they want to be *told* about it. They don't want to know if the change is good or bad until they understand it.

2. *Personal Concerns*—How will the change impact me personally? What's in it for me? Will I win or lose? How will I find the time to make the change? People with personal concerns wonder if they have the skills and resources to implement the change.

3. *Implementation Concerns*—What do I do first? Second? Third? How do I manage all the details? What happens if it doesn't work as planned?

Where do I go for help? How long will this take? Is what we are experiencing typical? People with implementation concerns are focused on the details involved in implementing the change.

4. *Impact Concerns*—Is the effort worth it? Is the change making a difference? Are we making progress? People with impact concerns are interested in whether the change is paying off. This is the stage where team members sell themselves on the benefits of the change.

5. *Collaboration Concerns*—Who else should be involved? How can we work with others to get them involved in what we are doing? How do we spread the word? People with collaboration concerns are focused on coordination and cooperation with others. They want to get everyone on board because they are convinced the change is making a difference.

6. *Refinement Concerns*—How can we make the change even better? Can we improve on our original idea? People with refinement concerns are focused on continuous improvement.

To help people resolve the questions and concerns they have at each stage of the change process, it is most helpful to respond with the right combination of direction and support. By so doing, the questions are answered and people are prepared to move to the next stage of change. Not addressing the questions will hold people back and delay, if not stop, the process from moving forward. It is here that Situational

Leadership® II provides a framework that leaders and team members alike can use to help them provide what is needed at the right time, thus keeping the process moving forward.

A BRIEF OVERVIEW OF SITUATIONAL LEADERSHIP® II

Situational Leadership® II was created to develop individuals to their highest level of performance through effective one-on-one leadership.[2] It is based upon creating a match between an individual's *development level* (various combinations of competence and commitment) on a specific goal or task and the *leadership style* (various combinations of directive and supportive behavior) that the leader applies.

As illustrated in the model below, four basic leadership styles can be matched with the four development levels. The top of the model illustrates the four leadership styles—Style 1—*Directing* (high directive behavior and low supportive behavior); Style 2—*Coaching* (high directive behavior and high supportive behavior); Style 3 —*Supporting* (high supportive behavior and low directive behavior); and Style 4—*Delegating* (low supportive behavior and low directive behavior). These leadership styles correspond with the four development levels—shown on the development level continuum at the bottom of the model: Development Level 1 (low competence and high commitment), Development Level 2 (low to some competence and low commitment), Development Level 3 (moderate to high competence and variable commitment) and Development Level 4 (high competence and high commitment).

The goal of Situational Leadership® II is to provide an environment that permits an individual to move along the development continuum—through the development cycle—from Development Level 1 (developing) to Development Level 4 (developed). The leader uses a leadership style that is appropriate to the individual's development level at each stage of development *on a specific goal or task.* As the development level changes, the leadership style should change accordingly. There is no *best* leadership style because development levels vary from person to person and from task to task.

The Situational Leadership® II Model

(High)

SUPPORTIVE BEHAVIOR

High Supportive
and
Low Directive
Behavior

SUPPORTING

COACHING

High Directive
and
High Supportive
Behavior

S3 | **S2**

S4 | **S1**

DELEGATING

DIRECTING

Low Supportive
and
Low Directive
Behavior

High Directive
and
Low Supportive
Behavior

(Low) ━━━ DIRECTIVE BEHAVIOR ━━━▶ (High)

Developed ◀━━━━ Developing

INDIVIDUAL DEVELOPMENT LEVEL

D4	D3	D2	D1
High Competence and High Commitment	Moderate to High Competence and Variable Commitment	Low to Some Competence and Low Commitment	Low Competence and High Commitment

Adapted from Leadership and the One Minute Manager by Ken Blanchard, Patricia Zigarmi, and Drea Zigarmi (New York: William Morrow and Company, Inc., 1995) 56, 68.

DEVELOPMENT LEVELS AND LEADERSHIP STYLES

While many variables can affect an individual's ability to do a job well, Situational Leadership® II focuses on one variable more than others—the development level of a person on a specific goal or task. Development level is a combination of two factors—competence and commitment.

Competence is the knowledge and skills an individual brings to a goal or task. Competence is best determined by demonstrated performance. It can, however, be developed over time with appropriate direction and support. Competence can be gained through formal education, on-the-job training, and experience. Experience includes certain skills that are transferable from a previous job—for example, the ability to plan, organize, solve problems, and communicate well. These skills are generic by nature and are often an essential part of many different tasks.

Commitment is a combination of an individual's motivation and self-confidence on a goal or task. Interest and enthusiasm are exhibited behaviorally through attentiveness, animation, energy levels, and facial expressions, as well as through verbal cues. Confidence is characterized by a person's self-assuredness. It is the extent to which people trust their own abilities to do a task. If either motivation or confidence is low or lacking, commitment as a whole is considered low.

The development of an individual to his or her highest level of performance can be seen as a journey very similar to the journey to empowerment. Although the goal is self-reliance (being able to perform in an empowered manner), the individual has distinctive needs along the way, as his or her competence and commitment fluctuate before finally reaching high competence and high commitment.

In order to address those changing needs, leaders and team members can utilize various leadership styles, which can be defined as combinations of directive and supportive behaviors. When leaders perform *directive behaviors* they concentrate on *how* to do a task. Examples include telling and showing people what to do and when to do it and providing frequent feedback on results. Directive behaviors are instrumental in developing competence in others. When leaders perform *supportive behaviors* they focus on developing people's initiative and on their attitudes and feelings toward the task. Good examples of supportive behavior are praising, listening, encouraging, and involving others in problem solving and decision making. Support is instrumental in building commitment in others.

MATCHING LEADERSHIP STYLE TO DEVELOPMENT LEVEL

Situational Leadership® II teaches us that to get the best performance and to develop people's skills, you match the right combination of directive and supportive behaviors to address the person's current level of competence and commitment. The basic idea is that when competence for a task (such as acting in an empowered fashion) is low, the leader or another team member needs to provide a great deal of directive behavior. As competence for the task increases, the amount of directive behavior needed decreases. A similar relationship holds for commitment and supportive behavior. When commitment for the task is low (such as when someone becomes discouraged), the leader or another team member needs to provide a great deal of supportive behavior. As commitment for the task increases, the amount of supportive behavior needed decreases.

It is important to recognize that there are many combinations of competence and commitment that require a variety of combinations of directive and supportive behaviors. As an illustration, let us explore the specifics of the four development levels as they match the four leadership styles from the basic Situational Leadership® II model displayed earlier.

On new tasks where people have little, if any, prior experience, most individuals are enthusiastic and ready to learn (they are at Development Level 1—low competence and high commitment). Just consider how people must feel when embarking on a journey from a hierarchical-style organization culture to a culture of empowerment. Being empowered may sound great, but people have little experience with it. At this stage of development, they need a great deal of directive behavior but not too much supportive behavior. They are excited already; the most supportive action to take is to address their concerns for understanding what it means to become empowered and to begin teaching them the skills of empowerment.

Not too long after beginning the task of becoming empowered, people commonly experience a period of disillusionment. A letdown occurs because the task is more difficult or is perhaps different than expected. While they now have more competence than when they started the task, competence is still not very high, and the disillusionment that people experience causes a decrease in commitment. (They are now at Development Level 2—low to some competence and declining or low commitment.) At this stage of development, people still need a relatively high level of directive behavior, but now they also need a high level of supportive behavior. The supportive behavior can directly address the concerns associated with discouragement, while the directive behavior continues to work on increasing people's competence for this new task of being empowered.

As the journey continues, people gradually acquire the skills they need for the new task of being empowered. Unfortunately, most individuals experience self-doubt about those skills. They question whether they can act in an empowered fashion effectively *on their own.* (They are at Development Level 3—variable commitment and moderate to high competence.) At this stage of development, people do not need a high level of directive behavior since their skills are actually quite good. But they do need continued high supportive Behavior, since their self-doubt and lack of self-confidence limit their ability to use those skills effectively.

In time and with this proper support, people will become self-reliant, empowered team members. (They are at Development Level 4—high competence and commitment for the task.) At this final stage of development, people have arrived at the destination of empowerment. They need very little directive or supportive behavior, because they and their team members can rely upon their competence and commitment for empowerment to provide their own direction and support.

THE DEVELOPMENT CYCLE

Besides this concept of matching leadership style to the development needs of people, Situational Leadership® II helps us to understand the development cycle, or flow of concerns, needs, and appropriate leadership actions over the entire journey to empowerment. By matching leadership style to the development level (and thus addressing people's needs at each stage of the journey), leaders and team members help ensure that competence and commitment for the task of empowerment continue to move toward high levels. In other words, given the appropriate amounts of directive and supportive behaviors at each stage of the journey, people move from one level of development to another, from being (1) enthusiastic beginners for the empowerment task to (2) disillusioned learners about empowerment to (3) capable but cautious empowered performers to (4) self-reliant empowered achievers.

We can depict this development cycle as shown below, and we can also relate it to the stages of change from the previous chapter. As we travel through the three stages of change (please note that the diagram flows right to left for the stages), we are essentially moving through the first three development levels. By applying the right leadership style at each stage (development level), we can keep the process moving toward the final development level—the destination of empowerment—where people have high competence and high commitment for being empowered.

This diagram is also useful in highlighting a common mistake leaders make that can inhibit, and sometimes stop, the movement to empowerment. In order to move successfully along the journey, it is important to recognize that each of the three stages

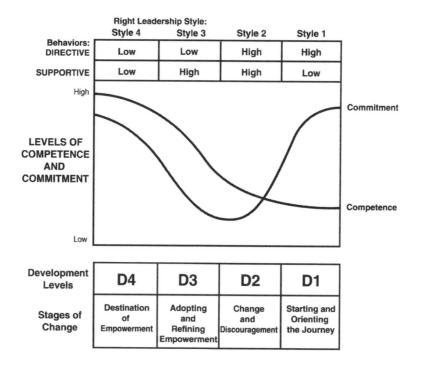

The Development Cycle
with
Leadership Styles and Stages of Change

Right Leadership Style:

| Style 4 | Style 3 | Style 2 | Style 1 |

Behaviors:				
DIRECTIVE	Low	Low	High	High
SUPPORTIVE	Low	High	High	Low

LEVELS OF COMPETENCE AND COMMITMENT

High

Commitment

Competence

Low

Development Levels	D4	D3	D2	D1
Stages of Change	Destination of Empowerment	Adopting and Refining Empowerment	Change and Discouragement	Starting and Orienting the Journey

must by addressed basically in the order shown in the diagram. The concerns that people have and the way they develop tend to occur in this order, and using the leadership styles out of order can create problems. Consider what a leader must do to help move someone from an enthusiastic beginner on empowerment to a self-reliant, empowered achiever. Leadership Style 1 is the most helpful for an enthusiastic beginner, and Leadership Style 4 fits an individual who has the necessary skills and confidence to perform well without supervision. What two leadership styles does the leader have to pass through to get to Style 4? The answer, quite obviously, is Leadership Style 2 and Leadership Style 3.

The problem with most leaders is that they do not "stay on the path" from one stage to the next. Some leaders do not even start with Style 1, preferring the destination Styles 3 and 4. But even those who start with directive Style 1—where they are clarifying the task before people, teaching new skills, and monitoring performance—often get derailed by jumping to a low directive and low supportive Style 4, where they essentially say, "Good luck!" This sets people up for failure since the leader does not work with the people as they move through the stages and experience various concerns and development needs. After a promising start, people are left on their own to figure out how to become empowered and how to deal with the discouragement that is a natural part of the process. For the empowerment journey to be successful, leaders need to stay on track with people as they guide them to the final destination—independence and a capacity to be empowered and to effectively use the new skills they have acquired.

APPLYING SITUATIONAL LEADERSHIP® II TO A SELF AND TEAM PERSPECTIVE

One of the most powerful aspects of Situational Leadership® II as a framework for guiding the empowerment journey is that it applies at the self-management level and the team level, as well as in the leader-member relationship. Perhaps you noticed throughout the previous sections of this chapter how we often spoke of leaders and team members. This was done as a subtle way of introducing you to the fact that Situational Leadership® II actually helps us recognize that empowerment is a partnership process between team members and team leaders (formerly called employees and managers in a hierarchical culture). For such a partnership to work effectively, all partners need to have access to the same set of analytic tools. When leaders diagnose the needs of team members, they will want to involve people in their own diagnosis. Likewise, when team members are feeling certain concerns, it is helpful if they can diagnose their own needs and ask for the appropriate amounts of directive and supportive behaviors.

SITUATIONAL SELF LEADERSHIP

To illustrate the problem that can occur when only one of the partners understands Situational Leadership® II, consider the following example. Suppose a leader has recently learned about Situational Leadership® II and is beginning to apply it on the job. The leader uses the model to diagnose one of the team members as someone who has the competence and commitment to do his job, including all the different tasks involved. As a result, the manager decides to use Leadership Style 4 (low supportive and low directive behaviors). Consequently, the leader leaves the person alone and seldom provides either direction or support. Since this direct report does not know Situational Leadership, how do you think this person will start to feel? Abandoned! The person might wonder, What did I do wrong? Why don't I see my manager any more?

Take another person who also works with this leader. The leader diagnoses this person as enthusiastic but inexperienced. Applying the model, the leader decides this person needs a considerable amount of directive behaviors. Every day the leader goes to see this person, gives directions, and closely supervises performance. After a while, what do you think this person will feel, not knowing Situational Leadership? Mistrusted! The person might wonder, Why is my manager always hovering around me?

And what if these team members meet in the hall one day. The first person we described says, "I wonder what happened to my manager; I never see her any more." The second person responds, "I know where she is; she's always in my office on my case."

What has happened is that the partnership process has failed. Even if both of these diagnoses are correct, the corresponding leadership style has been misperceived because of a lack of communication. What we have found over the years is that *Situational Leadership is not something you do to people; it's something you do with them.* This realization motivated Ken Blanchard, Susan Fowler Woodring, and

Laurie Hawkins to develop Situational Self Leadership.[3]

Situational Self Leadership is directed at individual contributors, although it also can be utilized by anyone in an organization who needs leadership from someone else. It helps people determine the kind of leadership (amount of directive and supportive behaviors) they need to accomplish a specific task or achieve a specific goal (such as becoming empowered). The focus is on what leadership style people *need* (from their perspective) to be successful in what they are doing. By teaching all team members, as well as their leaders, about Situational Leadership® II, the leaders and members can jointly diagnose the team members' needs and agree on the leadership style that the team leader needs to provide at each stage of the empowerment process.

SITUATIONAL TEAM LEADERSHIP

Another leadership domain that Situational Leadership® II can impact is team leadership. *A team is two or more people who must work together to accomplish a common purpose and are held accountable for the results.* As we suggest in the third key to empowerment (Teams Become the Hierarchy), empowered work teams are the means to meet today's demands for innovation, quality, service, productivity, and satisfaction. Working in empowered teams calls for new knowledge and skills not developed in most organizations in the past. As people spend more time in teams and move in and out of various team settings, they will be expected to acquire and carry specialized knowledge and skills with them. To meet these demands, people must be empowered with the critical knowledge and skills that make them productive members of a team.

The knowledge and skills required by all team members include the ability to observe and understand what is occurring in the team at any point in time and to intervene in ways that help the team grow and develop. This is where the work Ken Blanchard, Don Carew, and Eunice Parisi-Carew have done integrating Situational Leadership® II with team development concepts comes into play.[4] Using the same focus on direction and support that define the leadership styles, they provide a diagnostic model that matches the leadership style options to the needs that teams have at each of four stages of team development.

The four stages that teams must pass through to become empowered are based upon what happens to two key variables that are team analogs to the competence and commitment of individual development in Situational Leadership® II. First is *productivity,* which is the team's ability to work together and achieve results. Second is *morale,* which is the team's motivation, confidence, and cohesion.

The development of a team to the status of empowered team is a journey. Following a pattern similar to individual development, the team at each stage of development has distinctive needs.

STAGE 1: ORIENTATION

At this first stage (Orientation)—which parallels the first stage of the change-to-empowerment process (Starting and Orienting the Journey)—most team members think empowerment sounds good and are fairly eager to be on the team. However, they often start with unrealistically high expectations. For example, they often expect that the team will immediately be allowed and able to make all decisions affecting it. These expectations are accompanied by some anxiety about how the team members will fit in, how much they can trust others, and what demands will be placed on them. Team members are also unclear about norms, roles, goals, and timelines. Situational Leadership® II suggests that the team needs high direction and low support to address members' needs at this first stage. Typical behaviors at this stage include developing a clear team purpose, establishing clear roles for team members, setting goals for the team, and teaching team skills. Usually, these behaviors are provided by the team leader, though the door should be open for team members to contribute directive behaviors, as well.

STAGE 2: DISSATISFACTION

The second stage of team development (Dissatisfaction) parallels the second stage of the change process (Change and Discouragement). As the team gains some experience, morale dips because team members experience a discrepancy between their initial expectations and reality. The difficulties in accomplishing the task and in working together lead to confusion and frustration, as well as a growing dissatisfaction with dependence on the leadership figure. Team members develop negative reactions toward each other, and subgroups form, thus polarizing team members. The breakdown of communication and an inability to problem solve result in lowered trust. Productivity may be slowly increasing but may be hampered by team functioning. Clearly the team still needs a great deal of direction, but they now also need support. Examples of behaviors that either the leader or team members can provide include revisiting team purpose, teaching conflict-resolution skills, actively listening, soliciting input from all members, and recognizing small team accomplishments.

STAGE 3: INTEGRATION

The third stage of team development (Integration) mirrors the third stage of the change process (Adopting and Refining Empowerment). As the issues encountered in the Dissatisfaction stage are addressed and resolved, morale begins to rise. Task accomplishment and technical skills increase, which contributes to increased productivity of the team and a positive, even euphoric, feeling. There is increased clarity and commitment to purpose, values, norms, roles, and goals. Trust and cohesion increase as communication becomes more open and task oriented. There is a willingness to share responsibility and control. Team members value the differences among themselves. The team members start thinking in terms of "we" rather than "I." Because the newly developed feelings of trust and cohesion are fragile, team members may avoid conflict for fear of losing the positive climate. This reluctance to deal with conflict can slow progress and lead to less-effective decisions. What the team needs primarily from team members is enhanced support combined with a decrease in direction. The team members know how to work together, but they are reluctant to fully employ all their talents. Examples of leadership behaviors that can help the team at this stage include encouraging full involvement by all team members, encouraging shared responsibility for results, examining team functioning to eliminate obstacles, and encouraging and valuing different perspectives on the team's tasks.

STAGE 4: PRODUCTION

This final stage of team development is analogous to the team reaching full status as an empowered team. At this stage, both productivity and morale are high, reinforcing one another. There is a sense of pride and excitement in being part of a high-performing team. The primary focus is on performance. Purpose, roles, and goals are clear. Standards are high, and there is a commitment not only to meeting standards but also to continuous improvement. Team members are confident in their ability to perform and overcome obstacles together. They are proud of their work and enjoy working together. Communication is open and leadership is shared. Mutual respect and trust are the norms. The team flexibly handles new challenges in its continued growth.

SITUATIONAL LEADERSHIP® II AND THE CHANGE-TO-EMPOWERMENT PROCESS

We started this chapter focusing on the six predictable concerns that people have during the change-to-empowerment process, so let us close by showing how new work by Ken Blanchard, Patricia Zigarmi, and Drea Zigarmi on Situational Leadership® II and change provides guidance for the actions that will address each of the concerns.[5] As shown earlier in the development cycle, the four basic styles of leadership from Situational Leadership® II (with differing emphases) match the development needs and stages of change that mark the journey to empowerment. Based upon the discussion of self-management, we can see how a partnership between a team leader and each team member is desirable. We can also see that the stages that teams must experience in becoming empowered teams can be guided with the right leadership style for each stage of development. In this final section, we will explore how this development cycle can also be applied to addressing the six concerns of the change process, thus providing an inclusive framework to guide your actions. All of these elements are depicted in the diagram below (again the stages flow right to left on the diagram). Let us now explain how the four leadership styles can help in addressing each of the six concerns of change.

The Development Cycle
with
Leadership Styles, Team Stages, and Concerns

Right Leadership Style:

	Style 4	Style 3	Style 2	Style 1
Behaviors: DIRECTIVE	Low	Low	High	High
SUPPORTIVE	Low	High	High	Low

LEVELS OF COMPETENCE (Productivity) AND COMMITMENT (Morale)

High — Low

Commitment (Morale)

Competence (Productivity)

Development Levels	D4	D3	D2	D1
Stages of Change	Destination of Empowerment	Adopting and Refining Empowerment	Change and Discouragement	Starting and Orienting the Journey

Refinement Collaboration Impact Implementation Personal Information

FOR INFORMATION CONCERNS, USE LEADERSHIP STYLE 1

In the first stage of change, (Starting and Orienting the Journey) people have knowledge and skills for the change (productivity, ability), but morale tends to be naively high. People have information needs. They want to know, What is the change all about? What will we be doing differently? They need direction much more than support. To guide the process, leaders should

- Identify desired outcomes and share an image of what a successful change to empowerment would look like;
- Provide an action plan to reduce the gap between reality and people's idealized concept of empowerment;
- Share information that clarifies where the organization is now and where it is going;
- Set up small experiments and pilots; provide credible role models;
- Provide information that allows employees to reach their own conclusions.

FOR PERSONAL CONCERNS, USE LEADERSHIP STYLE #1 BLENDING INTO STYLE 2

As knowledge increases, people realize they will need to develop new skills. Anxiety starts to increase. They want to know, How will the change to empowerment affect me personally? Will I be able to be successful being empowered? They still need direction, but there is a growing need for support. Leaders should

- Provide forums for team members to say what's on their minds;
- Provide encouragement and reassurance;
- Explain to team members why the change is important and provide consistent messages about the organization's vision, goals, and expectations;
- Provide resources that help resolve personal concerns—time, money, management support, clear goals and expectations;
- Provide opportunities for acquiring new skills needed to become empowered.

FOR IMPLEMENTATION CONCERNS, USE LEADERSHIP STYLE 2

In the second stage of change (Change and Discouragement), people realize they not only have to acquire new skills, they also have to use them effectively and, eventually, on their own. They begin to wonder how long this change will take and what the plan is for getting there. The questions people have at this point are, How do I act to be empowered? What do I do first, second, and third? People still need both direction and support to address these concerns. Leaders need to

- Align systems—performance planning, tracking, feedback, and evaluation systems—with the change;
- Offer perspective about how long the change should take and whether performance is on track;
- Provide training and coaching on how to implement the change;
- Respond honestly to the questions people raise;
- Look for small wins, recognize progress, and share excitement and optimism about the change.

FOR IMPACT CONCERNS, USE LEADERSHIP STYLE 2 BLENDING INTO STYLE 3

As the second stage of change winds down, people begin to see the payoff in using their new skills. They begin to feel more confident that they will succeed. They want to know, How are we doing on our journey to empowerment? Can we measure our progress to date? The need for direction can decline, but people continue to need support to let them know that progress is being made. Leaders and team members need to

- Collect and share information and success stories;
- Create rituals and events that anchor the change in the company's culture;
- Work with team members to restructure the work unit in ways that support the change to empowerment;
- Remove barriers or obstacles to implementation and facilitate problem solving;
- Encourage people to keep up their effort and desire to reach empowerment.

FOR COLLABORATION CONCERNS, USE LEADERSHIP STYLE 3

As people are firmly in the final stage of the change process (Adopting and Refining Empowerment), they can clearly see that their efforts are paying off, and they want to expand the positive impact on others. They begin to have more and more ideas that they want to share with others. The question on their mind is, Who else should be involved in our empowerment efforts? They need very little direction but continue to need support to encourage them to use the talents of empowerment that they have developed. Team members and leaders need to

- Build links between the empowerment change that is being implemented and other initiatives in the company;

- Encourage teamwork and interdependence with other teams;
- Cheerlead the increases in performance of the team;
- Encourage people to take on even greater challenges.

FOR REFINEMENT CONCERNS, USE STYLE 3 BLENDING INTO STYLE 4

The destination is now in sight. People know how to act empowered and how to work in empowered teams. They are ready to ask questions such as, Can we identify new challenges and think of better ways to do things? Can we leverage what we have done so far? The need for both direction and support is declining. The team members and leaders need to

- Support continuous improvement and innovation by the team;
- Encourage each other to continue to challenge the status quo;
- Encourage each other to fully release the knowledge and experience in every member of the team.

As teams reach the destination of empowerment, leadership from any one team member or leader can employ very little of either directive or supportive behaviors. Because the destination has been reached, the direction and support come from the team members and leader functioning as a collaborative unit. Empowered teams filled with empowered people are able to release the power within people to achieve astonishing results. Their only remaining concern—which is now more of a desire and a commitment—is to keep the empowerment culture alive and thriving.

SUMMARY

As we have seen, to understand the change-to-empowerment process, it is helpful to appreciate the concerns people have at each stage of the journey. Coupling this with Situational Leadership® II, we have a useful, overarching framework for building an action guide for leaders and team members that will assist them in reaching empowerment. With this framework as background for your understanding of the challenges and appropriate responses for action, we now turn to the three keys to empowerment from *Empowerment Takes More Than a Minute* and apply them to each of the three stages of the change-to-empowerment process. The next nine chapters will use this matrix of keys and stages to identify specific questions that people have asked us about the process and to provide clear action steps that should be taken within each stage of the change process. Creating a culture of empowerment requires more than announcing the destination. It takes an action guide to handle the challenges of the journey. So let us develop your action guide, beginning with Stage 1: Starting and Orienting the Journey.

STAGE ONE

STARTING AND ORIENTING THE JOURNEY

Given that empowerment (releasing the power within people) leads to astonishing results, leaders want to know how to start the journey to empowerment. Indeed, they usually want to know how to get there by yesterday. Unfortunately, the journey takes a little more time than that. This first stage of the process of changing to empowerment is filled with excitement combined with anxiety and a lack of knowledge of what empowerment means for the behaviors of everyone involved. According to Situational Leadership® II, this stage is a time for providing clear direction to focus people's natural but naive enthusiasm. There are many new skills to learn, and clear leadership is the key to meeting the needs people have.

In this section, we will focus on Starting and Orienting the Journey to empowerment. We will explore how each of the three keys to empowerment can help in meeting this initial challenge. Our format will be to pose questions that leaders often have about changing to empowerment and then provide one or more answers in short paragraphs. We will also insert examples from actual organizational experiences with the empowerment process. The first key we will focus on is information sharing, since it is the best way to really kick-start the process of change. We will then explore the other two keys to empowerment: creating autonomy through boundaries, and letting teams replace the hierarchy. Remember, it is vital to use all three keys to successfully move forward with the change to empowerment. So let us turn to information sharing as the critical first key in the process.

CHAPTER 3

Key #1: Share Information to Kick-Start the Process

Over and over, we have heard leaders and team members alike say, "Empowerment sounds great, but how do we do it; How do we start?" When we tell them they need to start by sharing more information, the response from leaders is often, "But we can't do that." And from team members, the response is, "What do you mean? We've never had much information before; why should we expect it now?" Such responses lead us to the first question that must be addressed.

Why Is Information Sharing the Critical First Step in the Journey?

1. The explanation is at the same time quite simple and very profound. If we want people on the front lines of companies to be responsible for making good business decisions, they must have the same information that managers use to make good business decisions. *People without information cannot make good business decisions,* nor are they motivated to risk making decisions in such a void. On the other hand, *people with information are almost compelled to take*

the risk of making business decisions to the best of their abilities.

2. The key point is that if we want people to take the risk of being accountable in making important decisions, they must feel they can trust management and the organizational systems. In hierarchical organizations, compliance is often rewarded more than is good judgment. Unless this relationship changes, talk of empowerment will be perceived as just another corporate lie. People will be wondering, What will happen if I make a bad decision but make it in good faith and with my best effort? If people fear the consequences (that is, if they do not trust the leadership), then they will not be willing to take the risk to make business decisions. It is safer not to act and just let someone else make those decisions—hence no empowerment occurs. But stop for a moment to think about the best way to build trust in an organization. What we have learned from experience is that sharing information is one of the most effective and simplest ways to kick-start the enhancement of trust. If a leader is willing to share the power that information represents, people hear—more clearly than any words can express—that this leader is reducing the barriers and including people into the circle of influence and involvement. This is especially true if sensitive information is shared. (We will have much more to say later about the type of information to be shared.)

3. Another factor that pushes information sharing to the forefront of the journey to empowerment is the need people have for direction, both individually and in teams, during the early stage of the change process. When we ask people if they would like to work in an empowered work environment, they are usually quick to give an affirmative answer. Then when we ask them how much experience they have had with empowerment, we often find they have had little or no experience in a culture of empowerment. What that means in terms of Situational Leadership® II is that *most people start the empowerment journey as enthusiastic beginners* (Development Level 1). They are excited about the prospect of making responsible business decisions but lack knowledge, experience, or the necessary information to do so right now. They need a leadership style with high direction, and if they do not get it, Situational Self Leadership would suggest they must feel safe enough to ask for the information and direction they need to start moving down the road to empowerment.

The same holds true for people working in teams. If they are to become self-directed work teams, they will start the journey in the orientation stage of team development, where they need a high-direction leadership style to provide the information and skills necessary to get the team started. Particularly, they need information to clarify the team's relationship to the organizational vision, purpose, and values.

4. The final reason that information sharing is the critical first step relates to our discussion in the last chapter of Situational Leadership® II and change. In any organizational change effort—not just changing to empowerment—people initially have a variety of information concerns that need to be addressed. Information sharing at this time will help people answer these kinds of questions:

- What is the change and why is it needed?
- What is wrong with the current situation in our company?
- What exactly needs to be changed, and what outcomes must be expected?
- How much do we need to change and how fast must we change?

Addressing the information concerns that people have during this first stage of change can provide them with the direction they need to focus their energy in positive ways. Particularly, this focusing leadership style (Style 1) should help people understand the desired outcomes and provide them with an image of what things would look like if a culture of empowerment was realized.

With this appreciation for why information sharing is such a critical first step, let us begin to address some of the other questions leaders have about using information sharing as they start the journey to empowerment.

How Does Information Sharing Address the Questions People Have When Change Starts?

1. Information sharing helps people understand the need for change. And when people understand the need for change, they develop a willingness that helps drive the process. Their attitude is no longer just "We need to change because someone said so." It becomes "We need to change because we have some problems that are affecting us all and that need to be fixed." With information, people will begin to understand where company, unit, and even personal performance need to improve for the company to become more competitive, and they will become motivated to use their knowledge and experience to work for improvement.

2. Do not make the mistake that many companies have made in trying to create empowerment. In short, do not start by giving people the big-picture vision of an empowered company that will be a better place to work. While their initial reaction may be positive, they will quickly lose focus because that vision will have no meaning to them. Remember, people initially have information concerns. *They are not yet ready to hear about the benefits and potential impact of the change. Only in the context of shared information will a vision*

of empowerment and its benefits become compelling.
Initially, people want to understand what is wrong
with the current situation and what must be changed
to fix it—information sharing sets the stage for that
to occur.

A New York-based cable television company
started its move to empowerment by creating a vision for the company and its future. Properly, the
leaders began to cascade the new vision down
through the organizational hierarchy. But very
quickly, they started to encounter problems. People
did not accept the new vision. Instead they had
many, many questions about why it was needed and
what it would mean to them. What became clear
rather quickly was that the people needed information to help them be partners in clarifying the vision;
they just did not know enough or trust the leadership enough to provide input into the vision-clarifi-
cation process. Their response was either "What is
this all about?" or "What is management trying to
pull now?" When the leadership was convinced to
begin sharing information about the company, its
performance, its market share, and its problems,
the process really moved forward. People felt they
could be players in the vision process, not just
spectators. Furthermore, information sharing enhanced the credibility of the leaders, because they
were willing to admit that their actions had not al-

ways been consistent with their stated values. Leadership's honesty and willingness to offer complete information made people want to participate and help improve the company's performance through the vision process.

3. There is a caution that you must keep in mind. Leaders must be careful to avoid misinformation. The information that is shared must create a realistic picture of the organization's situation. To filter information will only decrease the trust and credibility that accurate information can provide. In other words, tell it like it is. Do not hold back the bad news or embellish the good news. An interesting exercise to try is one we described in *Empowerment Takes More Than a Minute:*

Ask people on the front line to estimate how much of each dollar the company takes in drops to the bottom line after all expenses are taken out. You may be surprised at how much people will estimate. Estimates we have seen range from 30 to 50 percent, with few people realizing the number may be closer to 5 percent. This exercise helps people appreciate their need for information and the importance of their actions. They will learn that if they waste a dollar, the company must generate $20 in revenue to recoup that loss, and pay raises and other desired outcomes may be jeopardized because of waste—this gets their attention. Then, knowing that there are many ways in which money is "wasted," frontline people begin to get answers to two of the questions they have: What is wrong with the way things are now? and Why do we need to change?

What Information Do Empowered People Need to Help Improve the Organization's Performance?

1. Frontline people, supervisors, and managers from top to bottom of the organization need to understand the real objectives and workings of the business. They need to be told how the company generates money, what its expenses are, and how it makes a profit. Show them the operational figures, income statement, cash-flow statement, and balance sheet not only for the entire company but, perhaps more importantly, also for the division and site for which they work. The information must be meaningful to everyone and will therefore probably need some explanation during these early stages of changing to empowerment.

2. Teach people how to understand the company and its financial condition. Teach them how to read a balance sheet, an income statement, a

profit and loss statement. As an example, Educational Discoveries, Inc., in Boulder, Colorado, uses an eight-hour exercise called "The Accounting Game" to teach people the basics of accounting. Also, ask yourself as a leader what information you need to understand in order to know the business and to make good business decisions. Share similar information with your people. For example, reject rates, inventory turns, and customer complaints might be important to you. Then show people how their jobs relate to the numbers in these important areas and how they can positively impact these numbers through empowered (and improved) performance.

A useful tactic is to teach people about the numbers and then go through some "what if" scenarios to help them understand how their actions impact performance measures. For example, discuss the cost of rejects and then have them consider "what if" the reject rate increases from 5 percent to 7 percent—what impact will that have on profits? Likewise, "what if" we can reduce the reject rate from 5 percent to 4 percent—what impact will that have on profits? Such an exercise helps people begin to see how their efforts can impact company performance. They also begin to understand the need to act in a responsible fashion by using their knowledge and experience to make good business decisions

62

and to make suggestions for improving their own performance.

3. People throughout the organization need to be shown and taught about *sensitive* information related to company performance in order to develop trust and interest in the organization. By sharing realistic information (both good and bad), people will begin to set challenging goals that grow out of this information. Gradually, as they believe in the information's authenticity, they will want to use their considerable knowledge and experience to improve the picture drawn by the numbers. Just be patient since change from a hierarchical mind-set takes time and nurturing for both leaders and team members. Consider the following example:

In *Empowerment Takes More Than a Minute,* we used a modification of this real example. A mid-Atlantic-based information services company instituted a billing response center for customer questions. After six months of responding to inquiries that were often complex in nature, the people in the response center were told that their average response time was four days. Furthermore, they were told that the average response time in the industry was about two days. With this information and a sense of responsibility to improve, they were able, in about one month, to cut their response time to two days, but they were not satisfied. They felt they could still do better, and they continued to focus on reducing the response time. Over the next three months they were able to cut the response time to four hours on over 98 percent of the inquiries—from four days to four hours just because they had information and a reference point (the industry average) to give them a sense of reality. Indeed, information appears to be magical in how it motivates people to begin acting in an empowered fashion.

4. Be sure to also share information other than financial data. For example, share on-time performance ratios, absenteeism numbers, customer praisings and complaints, cycle time, individual and team goals, customer contacts and surveys. Also share departmental standings as measured by ease of working with other departments, community involvement, all information from employee satisfaction surveys, and what management is doing about points of contention, succession planning, training schedules, and whatever else leaders use to understand the business. Team members need the same information that leaders use to make good business decisions, and while it is not necessary to share it all at once, it is important to begin sharing important information right away.

Why Do Leaders Have Difficulty Sharing Information about the Business with Team Members?

1. Leaders often feel the information they have is either too sensitive or too complex for frontline people. We ask you to put the shoe on the other foot. How does it feel to you when someone tells you or acts as if "this information is either too sensitive or too complex for you"? We suspect you feel just like team members feel that those with information either believe you cannot be trusted with sensitive information or that you are too stupid to understand it or both—not a very empowering feeling. We suggest you start by sharing more information than you have shared in the past—maybe not everything at first, just more. Then you can see what happens. We believe you will be pleasantly surprised at just how responsibly your employees use this "sensitive information."

One company in the convenience store business demonstrated clearly what can happen when leaders withhold sensitive information. Each month the district managers came to the stores and told the store managers and store team members, "Sales are way below par; shrinkage (stealing) is way over stan-

dard." This was intended to motivate people to improve performance. There was only one problem:
they did not know what the standards were and
were not being given real information to measure
their performance. The only lesson they learned was
to get another job somewhere else. Contrast that
with another company in the same industry. Each
month the store manager had to explain the profit
and loss statement to the district manager at a
meeting involving all store team members. The
leaders and the team members had to explain any
occurrence that was below standard or above standard, and they knew the standards and controlled
the information with which to measure performance.
In addition, if a procedure was working in one store,
the store manager had to explain it to team members and leaders in other stores. The level of involvement and sense of ownership was incredibly different
than in the other company, and so was company
performance.

2. To further the change in your attitude about
sharing information, consider the following questions. Why would your people want to share sensitive information with your competitors? They
know that if your company loses business, they
may lose their jobs. Why would they jeopardize
themselves in that way? And if you are concerned
that your people will not understand why the

company makes so much money, remember the exercise about estimating how much money falls to the bottom line. They may already feel the company makes more than it really does. Surely you can explain to them the need to make a profit to reward the risk taken by those who have invested in the company. If you are afraid of letting your customers know that you make a profit from the products or services they buy from you, face reality! They already know you are in business to make money, and they too probably feel the company makes more than it really does. So how can it hurt if they know the real picture? Finally, your competitors already have a pretty good idea of what your company's profitability is; they are in the same industry and know the costs and margins just as you do. So go ahead and share the information; the risks are actually greater from not sharing information.

3. There is far more to be gained by sharing information throughout the organization than by hoarding it. By sharing information in small doses at first, you will see people grow in responsibility and accountability. You will also see them grow in their trust of leadership. Both of these outcomes will lead to team members feeling a sense of partnership and involvement and wanting to use information to improve company performance. And they will surprise you with positive results generated by their problem solving skills. Then

when they ask for more information, you will feel more comfortable sharing. The cycle will continue if you let it. You share information; team members use it responsibly; they ask for more information; you share more; they act with more responsibility, and so forth along the journey to empowerment.

A funny story illustrates how people with information can solve problems that often baffle management. An exclusive country club had a problem with members taking home the shampoo (which was quite a good shampoo) after their showers. The president had considered all sorts of options to stop the problem but had found no solution that would not offend the members. Finally, he shared this information with a locker-room attendant, who responded, "Don't worry, they won't do it any more." The president looked dumbfounded. The attendant continued. "It's simple. I'll just take the tops off the shampoo. No one will want to take the shampoo without the top!"

What Information Do Frontline People Have and Not Have at Present?

1. It is useful to compile a list of the types of information your people have at present and to com-

---

pare that list to the types of information leaders have at various levels of the company. Then ask yourself, What information are people lacking that would be necessary for them to make responsible business decisions? In other words, what information would be most important to start giving to frontline people? How will you teach them to use it?

2. Be sure to consider all the possibilities. Certainly consider revenue figures, costs, profits, reject rates, waste, quantities shipped, quality measures, and other measures of performance. But also consider information on how bonuses are calculated for leaders, how gain sharing works, how various financial ratios are calculated and used, and on and on. Remember that your goal is to give them as much information as you have for making important business decisions in a responsible fashion.

In our own company, The Ken Blanchard Companies, we make a point to share on a monthly basis sales, margins, and profitability. Anyone in the company (in the office or in the field) can access—via the internet—weekly sales figures by division, by district, and by salesperson. With this scorecard always available, plus the knowledge that the company has a profit-sharing plan, people throughout the company can act responsibly to help the company achieve its goals and, in turn, help ensure a profit-sharing payout. Yes, it takes effort to make this information available to everyone, but it is clearly worth it.

Where Is the Information to Be Found in the Organization?

1. Some leaders feel overwhelmed by the magnitude of the task of sharing *all* the relevant information that they use in making decisions about company performance. It is important to remember the flip side of what we discussed earlier. It is all right to go slow at first—you do not have to share everything at once. Indeed, from the standpoint of the frontline people, too much information too fast may make it difficult for people to begin using it effectively. Go slow at first, sharing some of the important information that you as a leader have available. Be sure to include training on how to find, access, and understand that information. Talk to the information services (or information technology) people in your company to discuss how to make the information readily accessible to everyone. With the power of technology today, there is no really good reason why people throughout the organization cannot have access to the same information, unless leadership hangs

onto an old hierarchical notion that people cannot be trusted with information about their company. We might add that team members will quickly see this reason behind their not being provided information that they know is available elsewhere in the organization.

2. It is important not to start with a plan that is too grandiose. You yourself will not believe in it, and frontline people and leaders will just roll their eyes, knowing it will not work and that you, as leader, will not stay with such a grand plan. Do not jump immediately to providing excessive amounts of information overnight, unless you want to create a great deal of frustration, irritation, and even distrust. It is far better to start with small amounts and build from there.

For example, some companies have taught interpretation of financial information using personal finances as a starting point that most everyone can understand. Everyone has to balance a checkbook and make some investment decisions, such as the purchase of a house; you can use these familiar scenarios to teach the basics of your company's financial information, while at the same time providing useful personal financial skills.

What Company Information Will You Feel Comfortable Sharing Immediately?

1. Do not expect yourself as a leader—or other leaders—to initially move too far out of your comfort zone in sharing information. Many leaders have spent their entire careers in climates where information was guarded by leadership and not shown to team members. We must not underestimate just how hard it will be to open the books to people. We recommend starting with the basics of costs and revenues and then moving into more detailed, complex, and sensitive information. Tell people what it costs to make one unit of your product or to provide service to one customer. Remember also that your people may have spent their entire working careers not expecting much information sharing from leadership. They will have to get used to the idea of having information that seems to compel them to be responsible. No longer can they go home at night and just forget everything. They are becoming partners because they now have the same information leaders have. Together, leaders and team members must learn to share and react to increased amounts of information that will

become increasingly more complex and more sensitive in nature.

2. We have said before that you must not filter the information, sharing only the good news or the less-sensitive information. But it is all right to start with some limits on the information to allow both parties to learn to work together in the context of increased information. And there may be legal limitations on which information can be shared even at later times in the journey, such as Securities and Exchange Commission (SEC) rules for publicly traded companies. If there are legitimate reasons that information cannot be shared throughout the company, be sure to explain to people why it cannot be shared. Be careful not to hide behind rules that do not really apply, just because you are unsure. It is better to express your reservations at this early stage and your desire to change your mind-set as time progresses. Likewise, if some information must be kept within the organization, share it with people and tell them why it is important to keep it among yourselves. Such honesty can go a long way toward creating a feeling of partnership between leaders and team members.

3. Recognize that if you want to change the attitudes of people, allow them to take on more responsibility, and be your partners in the business, you as a leader must change your attitude, too. Indeed, you may have to lead the way, given that

you have the perceived power that your people do not. Further, you have access to information that they do not have. The lead must be taken by you (at first), somewhat on faith, until the in-formation-sharing process begins to build the power of empowered team members working in partnership with their leaders and even with the top leadership of the company. And be on the lookout for another benefit of sharing information with people—they will very likely start to share information with you in return. We all know that your people have access to information you never see. When the process of information sharing is fully functional, the sharing will be flowing down, up, sideways, and diagonally in the organization, benefiting everyone with increased information and the knowledge it brings.

A humorous story illustrates the power of employee information. We were called in as consultants in a plant in the southern part of the country where turnover was running over 100 percent per year in a major hourly position. We said, "We would like to talk to the people in the area where turnover is the worst." The plant manager said, "Why would you want to talk to them? They're all leaving." We said, "Oh, we just have a hunch they might know something." Reluctantly, he let us visit with them. When we began talking to the people on the plant floor, we learned that they did not know turnover was over 100 percent, but they did know why. They said, "Six months of the year it's unbearably hot down here. The temperature often exceeds 100°F. We've been trying to tell the foremen for years, but they never listen to us." We trotted back up to the plant manager and recommended an improved cooling system. With the new cooling system in place, turnover dropped to 12 percent. The plant leadership thought we were geniuses, and the people wondered why it had taken so long to fix an obvious problem. Granted, this story may seem a little farfetched, but reality in many organizations may not be that different. What is it like in yours?

How Can You Begin to Share Information Now?

1. Try a variety of mechanisms for sharing information about company or location performance.

A number of companies we have observed put up scoreboards in the lunchrooms that are updated daily or weekly to show important performance information. Other companies hold meetings each month to share and explain information about relevant statistics and to answer questions. Some even encourage team members to present their unit's financial information for the current month. Still other companies that are more technologically oriented put information out on the company e-mail system; some even allow space for questions and then try to respond via e-mail messages. Others use department forums, internal focus groups, or team breakfasts where the team leader cooks and leads the sharing. Information about objectives can be shared via methods such as screen savers on computers, bumper stickers, payroll stuffers, spouse newsletters, and family forums.

Whatever method you use, be sure the information is as current as possible. Provide yesterday's sales, shipments, rejects, and so on. Also, be sure the information is as clear as possible, but expect and welcome questions, especially early in this process as people are still learning to understand financial data.

2. Share information starting on the very first day with all new members at a location, be they transfers or new hires.

One company we encountered shows and explains its balance sheet and income statement to new hires. Someone explains the data and what it means and explains that team members are expected to be responsible for positively impacting the numbers on these financial and performance statements.

3. Remember that it is necessary to maintain a balance between sharing and explaining how to interpret information while, at the same time, emphasizing that everyone is accountable for impacting results in the company. Make it clear that team members need to understand the information and then begin working to create positive results with the information now in hand.

What Level of Information Should Be Shared—Company Data, Site Data, Unit Data?

1. This is a key question. Is it better to share information about overall company performance (e.g., earnings per share, overall revenue numbers, overall company margins) or should the information focus on a specific location where the recipients work (e.g., number of units of product shipped from the plant, reject rates for the plant, revenue generated by the site)? The response is that *it is critical to share information that people can actively impact.* People impact overall company performance only indirectly. What they can impact directly is the performance at their specific

site; hence, this information will be more useful in generating a sense of responsibility in people.

2. Start by sharing the factors and relevant data that the site leaders look at when reviewing performance. What are they held accountable for impacting (e.g., waste, overtime, shipped quantities)? These same factors are the ones everyone at the site must be held accountable for impacting; hence, this is the kind of information they need. Once team members are given access to the numbers that measure site performance, they can begin to be held accountable and responsible. Leadership can now begin expecting people to act responsibly toward site performance, and indeed, these team members will want to help in solving problems and generating new ideas that positively impact the numbers. Remember, any number that is withheld from your people is a number they will have difficulty impacting, and indeed, will have little motivation to impact.

3. It is also very helpful to share information that compares your site or company with other comparable sites or companies. Such data helps people make sense of the information that they receive. If you tell them that their reject rate is about 1.5 percent at this plant, that may sound good to them. But if you indicate that other similar plants in the company have rates around .75 percent, their performance takes on a completely different meaning, one that will motivate them to take

steps to improve their performance. The point here is not to create competition between the plants as much as it is to give people a perspective on what their performance means and a motivation to improve.

What Type of Responsibility Are We Trying to Achieve with Information Sharing?

1. What we want to achieve is a feeling among frontline people that they are accountable for results that positively impact performance numbers; we want them to feel the same sense of responsibility that leaders typically feel. In order to do this, frontline people need the same information that leaders use to make important business decisions. When such information is shared with people, they often make statements such as "I didn't know our performance as a plant was so low," or "I never thought much about the fact that my performance directly affects the quality of our products and the margins we achieve." Such enhanced knowledge will significantly impact the feeling of responsibility of frontline people.
2. Remember that in order to achieve the impact on responsibility that is desired, it is critical to teach people how to interpret the information they receive. Do not just hand over the site-level performance data (e.g., profit and loss statement or

cost information) and expect people to understand it. You have to teach them the basics of the financial aspects of running *your* business.

A packaging company developed an ingenious way of teaching business fundamentals using a game the leaders developed. All the fundamentals of running the business were taught in about a day using this game: How does the business make a profit? What costs must be considered? What margins can be achieved and how are they affected? What about the payback period for investments? How do you use financial ratios to analyze a business? What is a profit and loss statement?

Once these basics are understood, further learning can take place in the information sessions that we recommend first be held in a town-meeting format. This format allows for a give-and-take of questions and answers during the information-sharing sessions. In these meetings, you can use what people have learned to analyze their location or division in your own company.

3. In order to build the kind of responsibility that is desired in an empowered organization, here is a useful exercise to ask frontline people at early information sharing sessions:

> "What do you think you could do better if you had more information like the kind we are sharing today? Is there additional information that would be useful for you to have? If so, what is it?" Get them to talk about how they would use this information to positively impact the performance numbers that you are sharing with them. Also ask them the flip-side question, "What information do you have that would assist others, including leaders, in working more effectively? And how can we begin to share that information in a meaningful and timely manner?"

A useful reference point for understanding how information sharing builds responsibility comes from the book *Gung Ho!* by Ken Blanchard and Sheldon Bowles.[1] In this book, the authors use the story of Peggy Sinclair and Andy Longclaw to expose three secrets to "turn on" the people in any organization. The three secrets and their key components are shown in the table below.

The first secret, *The Spirit of the Squirrel,* explains the power of helping people see that their "work is worthwhile," beyond making a profit for the company. Sharing information is critical to helping people see the impact of their work, beyond the day-to-day activities. It is also tied directly to the second secret, *The Way of the Beaver,* which focuses on people feeling in control of achieving their goals. With information in hand, people begin to feel this kind of control and responsibility. The third key, *The Gift of the Goose,* focuses on the power of people cheering each other on toward their goals. Here again, information sharing gives people the perspective of progress that makes this cheering sincere and not just a "feel good" action.

THE THREE SECRETS OF GUNG HO!

SPIRIT OF THE SQUIR-REL	WAY OF THE BEAVER	GIFT OF THE GOOSE
Knowing we make the world a better place	A playing field with clearly marked territory	Congratulations must be TRUE: Timely, Responsive, Unconditional, Enthusiastic
Values guide all plans, decisions, and actions	Thoughts, feelings, needs and dreams respected, listened to and acted upon	Cheer people's progress as well as the end results
Everyone working toward a shared goal	Feeling able to perform but also challenged	$E=mc^2$; Enthusiasm equals mission times cash and congratulations

Adapted from Gung Ho! by Ken Blanchard and Sheldon Bowles, (New York: William Morrow and Company, Inc., 1998), 170–176.

What Should Happen in an Empowered Organization When People Make Mistakes with This New Information but Are Trying Their Best?

1. You must let people know that taking action and making a mistake will be viewed positively in your empowered organization. You must convey to

people that mistakes will be viewed as opportunities for learning based on trying new ideas and not as opportunities for punishing failure. All too often we have found that people are ignored when they do a good job, even if it was in a new area where mistakes were likely. Then when they do make a mistake, the boom gets lowered on them with full force. In an organization learning to be empowered, we cannot afford this "leave alone—zap" strategy. We must encourage not only risk taking, but also responsibility for learning from mistakes so that they are not repeated. Especially in this early stage of change, there is no room for punishment. Learners who are punished do not learn the new skill; rather, they learn to avoid the person who can help them become better and take few risks for change. Only through making mistakes can people finally learn to be empowered.

One of our favorite stories from *Empowerment Takes More Than a Minute* involves a company that hung large placards around the plant that read "MISTEAKS are important." The point was to send a clear message that mistakes have a positive value in the organization. They are vehicles for gaining and sharing new information about what works and what does not work. Not making "misteaks" means people are not trying new ideas and taking the risks associated with positive change. They wanted to

> celebrate mistakes as opportunities to learn, and their placard sent a clear message to that effect.

2. The way you handle mistakes can either erode trust or build it to the levels needed in an empowered organization.

At a remanufacturing company, the new CEO was greeted at his first plant meeting by everyone wearing rainhats, raincoats, and galoshes—in spite of the fact that it was a sunny day. Trust was so low in the company that no one believed useful information would be shared at the meeting; hence they came ready for another snow job from the leadership. By sharing information openly, both good and bad, and by working with people when mistakes were made (rather than punishing them), this situation was gradually corrected, resulting in outstanding company results.

How you handle the inevitable mistakes of people who are in the early stages of becoming empowered will send loud and clear messages about what is behind the efforts to empower people in the company. Do not fall prey to the tendency to be disappointed with mistakes and to take out this frustration on the frontline people who are acting in good faith to be empowered.

84

> In a retail company we found an interesting and powerful response to mistakes. In the words of their team members, "When we make a mistake, the boss instead of jumping all over us asks, 'What was your business reason for this decision or action?'" If a person shows logic and thought behind the decision, or that he or she had the company's interest in mind, the boss will always back that person and help him or her learn from the error.

3. On the other hand, do not teach only when mistakes are made. Be sure you recognize and acknowledge new actions by people that demonstrate they are taking responsibility for results and are having a positive impact on those results. In the early stages of empowerment, even little changes that signal people are taking responsibility for attempting to impact performance must be noticed. That recognition will encourage people to take more of these actions, hence teaching people what empowerment looks like. As your organization begins to move toward empowerment, do not be afraid to "catch people doing things right." If you celebrate learning and early signs of using information to act responsibly, you will see the empowerment process move into high gear.

CONCLUSION

We have presented many ideas and answers to questions related to using information sharing in order to get the empowerment process oriented and started. Before we turn to the next chapter, it is important to restate that information sharing alone will not get you to empowerment. It takes all three keys working together. We will, therefore, turn to how declaring the boundaries for empowerment can help in Starting and Orienting the Journey to empowerment.

CHAPTER 4

Key #2: Declare Clear Boundaries to Begin Creating Autonomy

Once information sharing has "primed the pump" for change by enhancing both the feeling of job ownership and responsibility in team members and the trust between leaders and their people, it is important to recognize the need to provide boundaries for acting in a culture of empowerment. Most people have an initial excitement about empowerment and the expectation to use good judgment, but they do not fully understand what that will mean or what to do. According to Situational Leadership® II, high levels of frustration and/or apathy will quickly follow initial reactions if there are no boundaries that provide direction for acting in a culture of empowerment. Before we talk specifically about the what, when, where, and how of boundaries, it is helpful to appreciate the magnitude of the journey to empowerment.

What's the Difference between a Hierarchical Culture and a Culture of Empowerment?

1. Let us start by explaining an exercise that helps people get in touch with the "break from history" that is created when we change to a culture of empowerment. People need to appreciate the magnitude of changing from a culture that is hierarchical to a culture of empowerment, and this exercise can help.

Show people a list of words that are typically used in a hierarchical culture, paired and compared with words that are typical of a culture of empowerment.

Hierarchical Culture	vs.	Culture of Empowerment
Planning		Visioning
Command and control		Partnering for performance
Monitoring		Self-monitoring
Individual responsiveness		Team responsibility
Pyramid structures		Cross-functional structures
Workflow processes		Projects
Managers		Coaches/team leaders
Employees		Team members
Participative management		Self-directed teams
Do as you are told		Own your job
Compliance		Good judgment

Have people discuss the kinds of attitudes and behaviors that are consistent with the words in each culture. The usual responses will be that in a hierarchical culture, people tend to do what they are told, avoid mistakes, shrink away from responsibility, boss watch, blame others for problems, and feel competitive with others in their organization. On the other hand, in a culture of empowerment, people tend to do what they see needs to be done, take risks and learn from their mistakes, seek out responsibility, check their own work, seek solutions to problems, know when rules don't apply, and feel a sense of cooperation with others in their organization. What becomes abundantly clear from this exercise is the vast difference between the hierarchical culture and the culture of empowerment.

As a follow-up to the exercise, we usually ask the question, "Who needs to change in order to move to a culture of empowerment—leaders or team members?" Of course, the answer is that both leaders and team members must change or the movement to empowerment will stall out and stop. And it is safe to conclude that both team members and leaders have far too little experience with empowerment to simply begin operating as though they were empowered.

2. Unfortunately, too many empowerment attempts have failed because senior leadership decides that empowerment sounds good and announces that the company will become empowered. The front-line people get excited about the possibility of bringing their brains to work with them, but they do not know how to be empowered. In Situational Leadership® II terms, they are at Development Level 1 (high commitment to the task but low task competence). If they are working in teams, they are in the first stage of team development (Orientation). In both cases, they need high direction, but they receive little direction or support for the change from their leaders because the leaders often are unsure what to do to create empowerment. The tendency is to blame these middle managers for the problem, but it is really

a senior leadership issue. Senior leaders must not just announce the change to empowerment and then disappear. Rather, they must help these middle managers use the appropriate leadership style with both individuals and teams by declaring the boundaries needed for empowerment to work. They must also focus people's energy at the organizational level by ensuring that what gets measured includes rewards for those at all levels who use good judgment. Leaders must stay the course by being available with continued direction and with added support when people, individually or in teams, reach the disillusionment stage of the journey.

3. Without clear boundaries from the outset of the journey, one of two responses usually occurs, as may be apparent from the description of the exercise above. One response is that chaos breaks out, with people exercising the freedom they perceive comes with empowerment. This is followed by quick failure, with leadership jumping into a "fix the problem" mode. This perpetuates a hierarchical culture with its "leave alone—zap" approach to leading and prompts the conclusion that empowerment is a flawed concept. Another response, which is more typical, is that skeptical team members do nothing different. They assume that empowerment is just the next fad that will soon pass. Managers see this lack of action and conclude that empowerment is just another flawed

concept. What we know from experience is that managers throughout the organization must look at themselves and ask how they must change to become leaders who can address the competence and commitment needs and information concerns of people, and the productivity and morale issues of teams, as everyone moves from a hierarchy culture to a culture of empowerment.

4. These reactions to change can be traced to the lack of knowledge and skill people have for working in a culture of empowerment. Empowerment is a new world for most people, and their lack of empowerment competence must be addressed if the journey is ever to be completed. Setting boundaries is an important step in this process.

With this appreciation of the paradox of creating autonomy of action through new boundaries to guide action, let us turn to addressing some of the more specific questions people have about using boundaries to create autonomy, especially early in the journey to empowerment. As we do, please keep in mind that the intent of boundaries in a culture of empowerment is not to restrict action (as it is in a hierarchy) but rather to create freedom to act within defined responsibilities.

Why Are Clear Boundaries Helpful at This Early Stage?

1. An important lesson from Situational Leader-ship® II is that "it is easier to loosen up than tighten up." The natural tendency in moving toward a culture of empowerment is to provide less structure rather than more in the beginning. And yet, with few people having much experience in empowered work environments, that usually ends in disaster. When failure is obvious and the leadership begins to tighten up and dictate boundaries, people resent it, even if the boundaries are appropriate.

2. We always tell leaders that if they are not sure how to supervise people, it's better initially to oversupervise them than undersupervise. Why? Because if they are better than you anticipated and you loosen up some of the direction and structure, they will respond positively. They will be glad you noticed their skills and ability to operate more on their own. That is why the leadership actions suggested by Situational Leadership® II start the early stage of the empowerment journey with Style 1 (high direc-tion/low support) and move in order through Styles 2 and 3 (high direction/high support and high support/low direction) and before fi-nally coming to Style 4 (low support/low direc-

tion), which is appropriate for the empowerment destination.

What Kinds of Boundaries Are Needed and Most Effective at This Early Stage?

1. It is important to distinguish between boundaries of empowerment and boundaries of hierarchy. Boundaries that exist within a hierarchy and with which most people are familiar tell people what they cannot do. In other words, these boundaries constrain behavior. For example, think of sign-off procedures that dictate obtaining signatures before action can be taken. Now contrast this with boundaries of empowerment that clarify for people the range of actions and decisions that they can make. In other words, these boundaries guide actions and encourage people to take responsible action. For example, a clear value like *be responsive to customers* guides action but does not constrain people from taking appropriate action in a given situation. This philosophical difference is a critical one for both leaders and team members to understand. Think about what people need to accomplish, make that clear, and allow them the freedom to use their talents to achieve those goals. That is the goal of boundaries in this early stage of the journey to empowerment.

2. It is also important to clarify for people that they will not be making all the decisions for the company, especially at first. Team members and supervisory leaders new to empowerment (most of us) often mistakenly think that empowerment means they get to make or be involved in all company decisions. Conversely, senior leaders worry about losing control if people get to make, or be involved in, all decisions. When people find out later in the journey that they do not get to make all the decisions, they tend to feel betrayed and to doubt the empowerment process, often feeling that it, too, is just another management tactic to get more work done. Hence, it is crucial to clarify this issue up front, both to guide responsible action and to guard the trust that information sharing has begun to build.

3. Essentially there are two categories of decisions to focus on at first: strategic decisions and operational decisions. It needs to be made clear that strategic decisions will continue to be made by senior leadership. Senior leaders will decide what markets to serve, what products or services to provide, profit margins and prices, the mix of products or services, the financing arrangements, and so on. What team members will decide are operational matters, focusing initially on less complex and involved decisions but gradually moving toward more complex and involved decisions. For example, employees can initially be

asked to make decisions regarding safety and housekeeping, measuring the quality of their work, and measuring customer satisfaction relative to their work.

4. Explain to people about the business that the company is in and the purpose of the business beyond making a profit and return for shareholders. How do the company's products and/or services fill a need for its customers? Providing people with this big picture, which explains the importance and meaningfulness of their work, provides a crucial boundary to guide their actions day in and day out. As part of this process, it helps people to see how what they do fits into this big picture—in other words, what is their little picture within this big picture? How is the puzzle of the company's work supposed to fit together, and where exactly is their piece of the puzzle? A series of meetings that allows people to ask questions to clarify the vision and make suggestions is a very powerful way to both build a meaningful vision throughout the organization and to demonstrate the kind of dialogue between managers and employees that will convert them into team leaders and team members.

The leaders of one West Coast utility company were very concerned about cost control, since they were about to enter the world of a deregulated industry. They had made it clear to everyone that this was a priority since it was part of the corporate vision statement. When linemen, customer service representatives, and others began to ask what this cost control was all about, the leaders went through a process of clarifying with people what "cost control" meant to them in their jobs. They answered questions such as, What does cost control mean to a lineman? How does he/she impact costs? What does cost control mean to a customer service representative? How does he/she impact costs? With these little-picture guidelines in place, people throughout the company began to impact costs and to save the company significant amounts of money.

5. With the information in hand from the first step in the empowerment process, people are also ready to hear and understand the company's vision. This involves learning its purpose or mission, values, and image. As explained in the popular book *Built to Last,* a company that hopes to be effective in the long run must develop and adhere to a core ideology that explicitly spells out a set of core values and a purpose.[1] Of course, establishing a core ideology that guides people, plans, and actions takes a process that not only develops this ideology but also ensures that everyone in the organization can relate to it. The book *Managing By Values* explains how this process must be

A COMPELLING CORE IDEOLOGY

Is Proactive	Is Future Oriented	Inspires
Is about Being "Great"	Is Challenging	
Appeals to Lofty Values	Touches the Heart and Spirit	

Developed by a Two-Way Process

Top-Down, Values-Driven
Senior Leadership:
1. Clarifies purpose, values, image

2. Shares throughout organization

3. Asks groups for feedback, changes ➡ ➡ *Bottom-Up, Values-Driven*

1. Group, individual visions developed

2. Visions aligned in all directions

3. Visions anchored to current reality

4. Refines into final statement   4. Strategies developed to bridge reality

5. Shares and explains how supported

Adapted from Jesse Stoner and Drea Zigarmi, From Vision to Reality, (Escondido, Calif.: Blanchard Training and Development, 1993), 9, and Jesse Stoner and Drea Zigarmi, Creating Your Organization's Future: Building a Shared Vision (Escondido, Calif.: Blanchard Training and Development, 1993), 15.

top-down and values-driven by senior leaders.[2] The top leadership of the organization must take the initial step in clarifying the purpose, values, and image of what the company can become as an empowered organization. Next, groups throughout the organization are established to provide feedback, ask questions, make appropriate changes, and gain commitment. This step essentially creates a bottom-up, values-driven complementary step to the process, as shown in the figure below.[3] People throughout the organization are asked to create their own visions for the organization. Next, the task focuses on creating alignment among individual visions and between individual and organizational visions. Once this picture of the future is clear, the vision must be anchored in the reality of where the organization is now. In the case of a vision of empowerment, the current reality will be some form of hierarchical culture. Finally, strategies must be developed to build a bridge for people and the organization between current reality and the future.

6. Once there is agreement on the purpose, values, and image, a unified and clear commitment must be achieved throughout the organization. This will involve a communication process in which top leaders explain the key values that will guide individual, team, and organizational practices. They should also clarify how the purpose, values, and

image will guide their own behavior, as well as the behavior of everyone in the company, and they should make clear the expectation that behavior needs to align with these values. Aligning values, behavior, and practices is crucial here. A good place to start, of course, is with senior leaders themselves as models. A reward and punishment system to re-inforce expected aligned behavior must be evident at every level of the company. Unless this happens, people will see the statement of values as a lie from senior leadership. In addition, the exhibited values must be consistent with the message being sent via the shared information and other actions. For exam-ple, what message is sent if there is a stated value of cost control, and layoffs are followed by the president's showing up a few days later in a new sports car that people will assume is a company car even if it is not?

One company that exhibits strong values to guide behavior is W.L. Gore & Associates. It has four core values that are the foundation for all decisions and actions in the company. People are expected to ad-here to these values from top to bottom of the orga-nization. The four are simple but powerful guides of behavior:

1. Fairness—dedicate yourself to maintaining it
2. Commitment—if you make one, you keep it

x99

3. Freedom—grow beyond what you are doing today

4. Waterline—a hole above the waterline won't sink the ship

Waterline is the key value impacting empowerment. Gore associates are permitted and expected to make any decision as long as it is above the waterline. Alternatively, decisions *below* the waterline could put the company at risk financially or in terms of an important relationship and thus sink the ship.

W.L. Gore & Associates has used these core values to guide it to profitability for over 30 years and to annual revenues exceeding $2 billion.

A contrasting example that illustrates the difference between words and actions is from a convenience-store chain where honesty and integrity were stated values. A supervisory leader would sometimes show up at a store at lunchtime and tell the store manager to "stale out" a perfectly good sandwich so the leader could have it for lunch. That was a lie, and everyone knew it!

When Should We Start Using Boundaries to Guide the Change to Empowerment?

1. As people begin to receive important company information and feel the responsibility that goes

with its receipt, there is an immediate need to begin clarifying boundaries. People will want to know what to do with this new information, as well as how to interpret it. They may ask about the expectations for change that go with having access to new information.

2. As explained earlier, information sets the stage for a new sense of responsibility for people and for an enhanced trust between team members and leaders. More than in a hierarchical organization, people will want to know what to do to act responsibly with this trusted information. In order to avoid chaos and to make clear that apathy is not an acceptable response in the newly empowered organization, people need guidelines for action.

A service company started the journey to empowerment by trying to create a vision of a new organization culture. When the process broke down, the leaders revived it by sharing information about the company and its declining market share. As the information sharing began to build responsibility and trust, people started asking how they could help improve the situation—essentially asking for some guidelines or structure. When senior leadership responded by presenting the vision again and clarifying goals for improvement and discussed means to gain market share through enhanced quality of operation, people gained a clear idea of what they needed to do. The organization began to experience the empowerment they needed to correct their market problems.

Are There Some Work-Related Boundaries That Should Be Used Early in the Process of Creating a Culture of Empowerment?

1. Beyond the grander and longer-term boundaries such as purpose, values, and vision, it is important to build on information sharing and its ability to generate energy for action and desire for responsibility by declaring the type of boundaries that are familiar to people. An excellent place to start is setting performance goals for people. But now goal setting should be a collaborative process involving dialogue between team members and leaders. Mandates never work as well as agreements. In addition, for goals to be useful, meaningful, and motivating, each should answer five key questions that make goals SMART.

S=Specific: "What am I going to do?"

M=Motivational: "What's in it for me?"

A=Attainable: "Can I reasonably expect to achieve it?"

R=Relevant: "Why am I doing this?"

T=Trackable: "How will I assess ongoing progress?"

Since setting goals involves collaboration between a team member and a leader, there should also be a discussion and an agreement on how the leader will work with the team member to help achieve each goal with which that person is charged. This is where partnering for performance, the team member knowing Situational Self Leadership, and his or her supervisory leader being familiar with Situational Leadership are particularly helpful. This requires a team member to be able to assess his or her own task-relevant needs and then work collaboratively with the leader to identify which leadership style is needed to help the team member achieve the goal.

An interesting example of what can happen with clear goals and a clear working relationship for achieving them is the budgeting process. Typically, when budgets need to be adjusted, leadership tells people not only how much to cut but what to cut—usually items like training and travel but rarely items like utilities. In one company, the approach followed through on the concept of collaborative goals and collaborative solutions to problems. When the budget got tight, team members were given the facts through information sharing. For example, the leaders might say, "We are having a tough quarter and need to make a 4 percent adjustment to get our budget in line. What ideas do you have?" It was amazing how many times people came up with ideas for both cost cutting and revenue generation that the leadership had never considered. They might suggest using a different shipping process to cut down on overnight shipping charges, or as a way to add revenue, they might suggest follow-up calls after shipments to see if the customers needed anything else. Team members knew the goal and could act like owners, using their ideas to offer solutions.

2. Another powerful technique to help clarify responsibilities and priorities is the Performance Planner Top 10, a tool developed by John Carlos with his clients.[4] Essentially, it is a structured method for aligning the goals a team member perceives as important with the goals his or her leader sees as important for that person. The technique asks each person to list his or her top ten responsibilities; the leader does the same for this team member. Then they compare the lists and work to create comparable lists. The value of the pro-

cess is twofold. First, it creates the alignment of goals that leads to efficiently working on the right things. Second, the process for arriving at the alignment—a dialogue—builds trust between the team member and the leader and creates motivation for the team member to achieve the goals.

When we first use the Performance Planner Top 10 with our clients, some interesting learning occurs. Typically, when people list their top ten responsibilities and we compare these lists to the top ten lists leaders create for these people, the results can be quite divergent. The degree of agreement is often somewhere in the 25-30 percent range. Clearly, such lack of alignment creates several problems for the organization and usually reflects the pain a team member is experiencing, that is, what you hold me accountable for is not what you tell me. Items on the person's list but not on the leader's list may be time wasters for the team member. Or they may be items that should be on the leader's list. On the other hand, items on the leader's list that are not on the team member's list are fertile ground for the leader's disappointment and resentment toward the team member. A discussion between the leader and the team member to reach agreement on the top ten list can yield significant progress toward improved productivity and necessary accountability in a culture of empowerment.

3. At this early stage of the change process to empowerment, it may be difficult for people to identify very many goals. Still, with the new information in hand and drawing on their work experience and knowledge, they may very well have some good ideas for goals that will improve performance and lead to corporate goals and visions being achieved. We know from experience that people who produce good results while performing meaningful work feel good about themselves and want to take on more responsibility. It is certainly worth the effort to explore this avenue. Either good ideas will come forth (perhaps with a little prodding at first), which will be helpful in moving the empowerment process along, or less-effective ideas can become great learning experiences for team members and leaders alike. Leaders can explain why a suggested goal is not critical or does not follow from the information being shared, hence creating a technical educational experience for the team member and an interactional educational experience for the leader—both assisting in the movement to empowerment.

> In one trucking company, every department was asked to set two or three goals that, if accomplished, would help the company improve financially. This request tapped a powerful source of energy. The energy came from people feeling that what they did

counted for something bigger than themselves. In accounting, they set goals focusing on accuracy, accounts receivable cycle time, and processing efficiency. The truckers set goals on lower gas consumption, lower accident rates, or better maintenance of the trucks. By using information sharing, they could establish baseline performance for each measure, then set goals for improvement, and then take responsibility for getting the job done. In the early stages, the goals were sometimes set unrealistically or set on unimportant issues, but over time, the team members learned with the help of leaders how to set very meaningful goals. In so doing, a tremendous source of energy came from being involved in solving company problems.

What New Skills Must People Learn to Operate in an Empowered Culture?

1. As explored earlier, the skills needed in an empowered culture are quite different from those needed in a hierarchical organization. People must learn to be far more responsible and self-directed in an empowered organization. Hence, training must be an integral part of the change to an empowered organization. And if

training is a stated value, it cannot be an option. Leaders who do not support the training (for example, by pulling people out of training classes at the last minute) or the behaviors learned in the classroom must be coached to change their *own* attitudes and behaviors. It is not acceptable for a leader to say, "Training is great, but back here on the job, this is the real world and here we do it my way!" In moving to empowerment, training must result in new skills being used on the job, and this takes effort before, during, and after the training.

In an internet server company where we were conducting some training, we noticed that everyone seemed rather bored, so we asked what was going on. The response was, "We're here to get our ticket punched to prove we went to a customer service program." We asked, "Don't you have to do anything differently when you go back to the job?" They said, "Oh no. We just have to prove we were here!" We felt like saying, "Well, you've already signed in, which proves you were here. You can leave now." Instead we began to discuss with this group what might happen if they did use some of the ideas we were teaching. A fruitful discussion followed, but the training was not as effective as it could have been.

To reach empowerment, training must look very different from the above example. People must come to the training knowing why they are there and what they are expected to learn. After the training, leaders must ask, "What did you learn? Now let's talk about how you can help others learn it and how we can begin to use the skills here on the job." The key issue is responsibility for learning and changing. Without that, empowerment will never happen.

2. Some specific skills related to the information people are receiving will be essential. For example, asking people to interpret and utilize information about the business requires that they learn what this information means. They will have to learn basic accounting practices and means for measuring the effectiveness of a manufacturing or service organization. Unless people learn how to interpret such information, it will, of course, be useless. Worse, it may make people distrust the organization and the top leadership even more.

One company in the food manufacturing industry contracted with a local university to provide basic business skills training on company time for all of its people. Professors from the university came to the company location once a week to teach people about accounting, finance, economics, manufacturing, and quality. These presentations were supplemented by discussions revolving around real company data prepared and presented by company leaders.

3. As new partners in the business process, people at all levels of an organization must also be taught the basics of business as it is conducted in their company. They have to learn how revenues and profits are calculated and reported in typical financial reports used by the leadership. They have to learn what market share means, how return on assets is calculated, and for what this information is used. They must learn how to interpret data on percentage defects or error rates and how to read production data charts and graphs. They must learn the difference between service and services. They must learn how to measure customer service from the customer's point of view instead of the marketing department's viewpoint. Business partners must share the same information if they are to partner in the critical operating decisions of the business. Ask yourself, What information do I have as a leader that team members do not have? How can we teach the people what this information is and how to use it to make important business decisions?

4. Keep in mind that people in the empowered culture you are trying to create do not want to look or feel stupid. Leaders who feel stupid take it out

on their people, and when we make people feel stupid, they have many ways to get even. Is this what we want—people who think their main job is to get even with the company, or leaders who feel they must take out their frustration on their people? Of course not. We want people who are excited about performance, productivity, and accomplishment, and we want leaders who relish working as partners with people. Both leaders and team members want to know clearly what is expected of them and how they will benefit from acting in an empowered fashion. Their fear will be that they will lose out in the new empowered culture, and this fear will perhaps be even greater for middle managers and supervisory leaders than for team members. There is a need to design training to teach both team members and leaders what they must know to succeed in an empowered culture. Since working in an empowered culture is like taking on a new task for which people have little experience and skill, training must be designed to raise their level of knowledge for working in this new arena.

5. As you continue to add depth of understanding to the analyses people conduct, remember that even middle managers may not always understand information on a company report well enough to explain it to their people. It is one thing to read and understand a report for yourself. It is quite another to be able to explain to others how to

use and interpret the information on a company report. Middle management leaders must be trained in how to be teachers of ideas and skills. Their job is changing to one of coach, teacher, and mentor, and many middle managers will not have gained these skills in the hierarchical setting from which they came. As we all well know, teaching others how to do something is far different from doing it ourselves—teaching requires the use of different skills from performing a task.

What Are the Expectations for New Decision Making by Employees?

1. The focus for people throughout the organization will *not* be on making strategic decisions for the company. They will not be asked to decide on new markets to enter, new products to introduce, or new production techniques with large budgetary implications. Instead, people throughout the company will be asked to focus on how to improve operations in ways that cut costs, reduce defects/errors, enhance quality, reduce downtime, and so on. And there will be a need to explain that improving such operational matters is a clear expectation for everyone, not just "nice to do if you have time" Eventually, this will require a reward and punishment system that supports and reinforces these efforts.

2. People will want to know what they can and cannot do during these early stages of the change to empowerment. Indeed, they must be told clearly what they are expected to impact as the move is made to empowerment. Top leadership needs to clarify the biggest operational improvement needs facing the company and state these as initial boundaries within which people need to focus their energy. Are the greatest needs for improvement in the area of cost control, improved quality, reduced waste, or decreased downtime? By spelling out these focal points, people will be able to take action that yields results by using their knowledge, experience, and motivation to address important business needs. At the same time, such guided action will prove to everyone—leaders and team members alike—that empowerment will really work for the organization.

3. It will be helpful to provide a list of prioritized needs upon which people can focus. This will guide them not only in their first empowerment pursuits but also in those efforts that are to follow in the early stages of the change process. It will also be helpful to provide a sense of structure by clarifying where people should go for help when they are unsure of next steps or of their solutions to problems that block improvement. Such guidelines will put the responsibility for action in the hands of the people. They will also encourage a dialogue around actions and decisions between

employees and managers, which is a key to the continued building of trust and moving to true empowerment.

4. It is helpful to define small but important decisions that people can make in the early stages of the movement to empowerment. It is necessary to focus on decisions that are, by nature, in the scope of people's daily work activities. They should be encouraged—indeed, expected—to make decisions about how they schedule their work, what they will do to impact the quality of their efforts, how they will maintain a safe work environment, what their daily goals will be, and so forth. Such decision-making actions will help people build their skill and confidence in making important business decisions and will prove to the leadership that people can make responsible business decisions when given information and some guidelines for action.

One of our colleagues in Australia, Trevor Keighley of PTD Group, Ltd., has developed a tool known as the Self Direction Assessment (SDA).[5] It provides a framework for selecting the smaller, less complex decisions early in the empowerment process and then moving gradually to larger and more complex decisions as the process unfolds. This tool has been used very effectively with organizations as a structured way to provide ever-expanding guidelines for autonomous empowerment. The tool is also team based, which ties into the next key that we will discuss—developing self-directed teams to replace the hierarchy for decision making and support for all members of the organization.

5. People throughout the organization will want to know how the change to empowerment will impact them personally. A discussion about the types of decisions they can make is a very concrete way of explaining this impact. It clarifies the range of autonomy people will have initially. It also helps to clarify the scope of responsibility and the risk they are being asked to take in the new empowerment culture. Since true responsibility and the potential of risk are new to people, it is important to start small and build to larger ranges of responsibility as the confidence of team members and leaders increases. Over time, the complexity and scope of the decisions people will be asked to make will expand, but for now it is important to keep the decisions less complex and impactful. We have to learn to crawl in an empowered culture before we can walk, and certainly before we can run.

6. Early in the transition to empowerment, we must teach people the skills of problem analysis and decision making that effective leaders use in the organization. How does one break down the

essence of a problem to get to the core cause? How does one consider alternatives in a way that is thorough without being too slow? How does one weigh the alternatives and assess which one has the best potential to yield the desired result? By acquiring and enhancing these skills through-out the organization, you are preparing people to make the best use of their knowledge and experi-ence, while enhancing the performance potential of the organization.

CONCLUSION

At this point we have begun to combine the power of information sharing with the power of creating au-tonomy through boundaries. The empowerment pro-cess is capable of moving forward, but recall that we said it takes all three keys to make the process really work and to reach empowerment. Let us therefore turn in the next chapter to how replacing the hierarchy with self-directed teams complements the first two keys discussed and how they all work together to start the process moving during this period of Starting and Orienting the Journey to empowerment.

CHAPTER 5

Key #3: Begin Developing Teams to Replace the Hierarchy

In beginning the journey to empowerment, it is important to remember that all three keys are crucial for effectively creating a culture of empowerment. Information sharing sets the stage for change, while boundaries provide the framework for acting with autonomy. What is missing, to truly get the journey going, is a mechanism that uses human interaction to provide the direction and support needed to best use and develop the talents that people have and will acquire. Self-directed teams provide the vehicle for this missing human interaction.

Teams help people address some of the personal concerns they have at this early stage of the process of changing to empowerment. People will have questions such as,

1. How will we deal with the impact that the change to empowerment will have on us?
2. Can we win in this new culture?
3. What will be different as a result of these changes?

4. Will we get the training we need to be effective in a culture of empowerment?
5. When we encounter problems, who will we turn to for help?

While teams can provide answers to these questions, it is important to know that teams—especially self-directed, empowered teams—take time to develop. Hence, in this early stage of Starting and Orienting the Journey to empowerment, we cannot initially expect great results from the teams. An effective leader who guides and develops the team may still be important in this early stage of change. We know from our discussion of Situational Leadership® II and teams in chapter 2 that teams go through four distinct stages in the development process. First is the team development stage of Orientation. Here the level of capability, related to "how to work together as a team," is low, while the level of team morale to "work together as a team" is naively high. The team needs a great deal of direction, particularly in clarifying its purpose, values, roles, goals, and operating procedures. This is the team development stage that is prevalent during the first stage of the change process (Starting and Orienting the Journey). Let us consider some of the questions people typically have about teams at this early stage in the empowerment journey.

Why Are Teams So Crucial to the Success of Empowerment Efforts?

1. The bottom-line answer is that empowered teams can do far more than empowered individuals. People are often skeptical about this comment because they remember their experience on project teams where some team members did not carry their share of the load, thus putting additional work on other team members. Situations like this occur because the people are a "group," not a "team." The difference is that a group is a set of people who have not developed a common purpose and likely do not know how to work together as a cohesive unit. A team, on the other hand, has a charter and is made up of people who have developed that common purpose and know how to work together as a cohesive unit. An example is a set of people flying together on a plane trip across country. If all goes well, they are a group only loosely connected by virtue of being on the same aircraft. But if the plane goes down in a remote location, the people are presented with a common purpose—survival—and how well they work together as a team will likely determine their fate.

An outstanding way to prove the point that teams outperform individuals is to engage people in an exercise like Desert Survival, Wilderness Survival, or Lost on the Moon. Each of these exercises has people rank a number of items in the best order for their survival after an accident has occurred. First they rank the items alone as individuals; then they rank them as a team. Both rankings are compared to the rankings of an expert, allowing a numerical score to be calculated to assess performance of the individuals and of the teams. The teams almost always outperform the individuals and, if they do not, the reason can usually be traced to poor functioning of the team.

2. Teams are crucial to empowerment because they bring a diversity of ideas and experience to bear on the complex problems that organizations face in the competitive and changing world of business. Collectively, the team of people knows far more than any individual on the team. We like to say that in a real team, "No one of us is as smart as all of us." Indeed, the team may know more than the best individual on the team, yielding a synergy (1+1 is greater than 2) that creates some exciting methods for solving important production, quality, service, and financial problems. Furthermore, teams can implement complicated solutions to problems, as in the outdoor challenge activities for team building, where a team of people can carry a heavy load, move their members over a

barrier, or provide assistance for everyone in getting through a difficult experience. The challenge is to get a group of people to become a high performing team. According to Don Carew, Eunice Parisi-Carew, and Ken Blanchard, high performing teams have the following characteristics that can be described by the acronym PERFORM:[1]

P=Share a common *Purpose*

E=Are *Empowered* to use the talents of all team members

R=Use *Relationships* and *Communications* effectively

F=Demonstrate *Flexibility* in making and implementing decisions

O=Hold themselves accountable for *Optimal Performance*

R=Provide *Recognition* and *Appreciation* for each other's contributions

M=Experience high *Morale* by feeling both the pressures of management and the pride of ownership

In essence, this PERFORM. acronym describes a team operating at the fourth stage of team development—Production. Unfortunately, there are two team development stages (Dissatisfaction and Integration) that must come first.

Can We Expect Teams to Be Immediately Successful, and If Not, Why Not?

1. Teams will have limited success in the early stages of moving to empowerment, but that is not to say they will have no success. There is often an untapped power in the joint abilities of people that can be released in the empowered team context. The power of teams can be truly amazing, but until teams have had the time to develop through the early stages of Orientation and Dissatisfaction, they will not be that effective. Just like a sports team or a ballet corps, it takes practice together to learn how to perform as a team and to gain a clear understanding of each other's roles. As long as you do not expect immediate miracles with teams and do make the time for training and practice, teams will become a powerful source of direction and support for all members of the organization.

2. Teams cannot be highly effective immediately because team members and leaders are coming from hierarchical organizations where decisions are made by managers and carried out by employees. Hence, team members will not be accustomed to making and implementing decisions or taking responsibility for the results achieved. Likewise, leaders will not be accustomed to al-

lowing and expecting people to make and implement decisions or to having them take responsibility for their results. Indeed, leaders may fear a loss of control by allowing teams to make important business decisions, but leaders may also feel they are shirking their responsibility by expecting employee teams to make those decisions. There are many old hierarchical scripts that will be playing in the minds of both team members and leaders, and these old scripts will inhibit team action. There is real potential for chaos and bad decisions as people embrace the changes at different rates, but more likely, there is the possibility for tentative action. Hence, it is better to expect small steps by teams and team leaders in this early stage of change. Even so, teams can begin to pay big dividends (albeit in small increments of continuous change) while developing their skills and preparing to take on bigger and bigger challenges.

In one company in the financial services industry, the initial efforts to use teams met with some serious difficulties because the leaders expected too much too quickly. In addition, they did not share enough information, nor did they provide enough guidelines for the teams to operate. The result was frustration on the team members' part and blaming of the leaders for creating an impossible situation. At the same time, the leaders became disenchanted with the whole team concept and were about to abandon the idea. They then realized what they had done and instituted team training for both managers and employees to help in the transformation process to team members and team leaders. The progress was slow, but positive results began to appear after several months of concentrated training.

3. As people begin to appreciate the power of teams, they will also realize that they do not have the skills necessary for working effectively as empowered teams. In a sense, they must unlearn the skills needed to work effectively in a hierarchical organization and learn new skills for working as teams of people. And this learning process takes time. A good place to start is with classes using experiential exercises to teach the skills of teams, followed by application on the job. But this means that the leaders, too, must be taught how to lead and develop teams. Managers who become team leaders must be willing to lead the teams to the point at which they can function without the manager, as the manager becomes a team member, too. Leaders must also remember that people cannot learn from experiences they are not having. At this early stage of the journey, the critical activity is for the team leader to create opportunities for people to accomplish tasks in the team rather than in the hierarchy. This, of course, means that leaders and team members

124

both must learn what teamwork means and how to be a good team member.

4. Two of our colleagues, Eunice Parisi-Carew and Don Carew, have found that teams in this early stage of development can be helped by going through what is called a team chartering process.[2] This extensive process helps the team its clarify vision, purpose, and values as they align with the organization's vision, purpose, and values. The team also clarifies its norms and ground rules for working together, as well as the individual task roles for each member of the team. The process also guides the team to clarify key responsibilities and goals for the team and for each member of the team. Communication strategies are also spelled out, along with decision-making processes and authority and accountability relative to all decisions. The final part of the charter specifies the resources that are needed by the team. This chartering process helps teams progress toward empowerment, though the charter must be regularly revisited to keep the focus clear and to make necessary adjustments. Still, the team can move rapidly through the Orientation and Dissatisfaction stages because the charter helps the team to quickly address ways to increase team productivity. This success helps the team avoid a serious drop in morale during the Dissatisfaction stage.

What Skills Must the Team Members Be Taught to Become Empowered Teams?

1. It is crucial to let people know that the issue in team training and practice is not whether they possess the technical skills to do their jobs. Of course, everyone needs to continually learn new technical skills, and most companies try hard to provide opportunities for people to learn those skills. The issue here is teaching people "how to manage themselves." It means helping people learn how to act as business partners who are accountable for results and who feel a strong sense of ownership.

2. Essential to the effectiveness of self-directed, empowered teams is learning how to make consensus decisions as a team. Most managers and employees do not really understand what consensus decisions are. They confuse them with unanimous decisions, or they feel that they have had no input unless the decision made is the one they suggested. Team training has to help people understand that consensus decision making means people might, even after extensive discussion, still have different opinions about the best solution to a problem (such that a vote on options would not be unanimous). In spite of those differences, everyone is willing to get behind one

option to do everything he or she can to make it work. Paramount in this communication phase is that team leaders must create a safe environment, where people can say whatever it is that needs to be said with no fear of reprisal. Leaders must learn the difference between a team member expressing a feeling or opinion that is divergent from that expressed by others and a team member expressing a refusal to support the team's decision.

One of our client companies had a CEO who always said, "Talk back to the boss!" But the people discovered that when anyone disagreed with the boss he or she was not included in future meetings. Once, a vice president stated that the marketing plan for the quarter was bad and would shred gross profit margins and destroy the required product mix. That was an opinion. The CEO treated it as a refusal to take part and fired the vice president. The vice president was correct, the company suffered greatly as a result, and the sharing of diverse opinions was clearly suppressed. Obviously, this CEO had a great deal to learn about consensus decision making and the utilization of different opinions to build a consensus.

3. For the team process to be effective, people must develop good communication skills *in a team setting,* which can be quite different from one-on-

one communications. The skill of listening to multiple ideas and assimilating those ideas into a whole is complex in a team context, especially where people have different ways of presenting their ideas. Discussions are often nonlinear, in that comments do not build on what was last said but may build on a comment made much earlier. Likewise, learning how to interject one's ideas so they are heard and considered is a unique skill in a team context. It is easy to lose your own idea in an involved discussion, even though it may be a great idea. Hence, remembering good ideas and timing the presentation of ideas become exceedingly important in team meetings. All of these communications are made far more complex when team members are geographically dispersed and/or when team members do not meet frequently. Communication skills must be a constant focus of moving a group of people toward becoming a self-directed, empowered team.

It is most helpful to have people go through a simple exercise of drawing the possible subgroups for different-size teams. Have them draw two people and then the number of subgroups—there is one. Now have them add a third person and then draw all the subgroups, including one-to-one and one-to-two links—here there are six. Add a fourth person and the number of subgroups jumps to eleven since

128

> we now must add the three one-to-three links. Very quickly the number of links becomes overwhelming. For example, with eight people, the number of links jumps to 247, and with sixteen people it is 65,519. The point becomes clear that communications in a group is far more complex than in a one-to-one relationship, but it is far richer. The key is to develop the skills to communicate effectively in this new context.

4. All team members must be taught the skills of planning and conducting an effective team meeting. It is not enough for the team leader to know these skills. When everyone knows the skills of preparing an agenda, running a meeting by the agenda, and providing follow-up to the meeting, then everyone can take responsibility for ensuring that team meetings are effective. Everyone can share the three key tasks of agenda preparation, meeting conduct, and follow-up. These same skills can also make conference calls, videoconferences, or electronic meetings far more effective.

5. Help people appreciate the benefits of working in teams. Both team members and leaders need to understand and believe that teams can fill many of the voids left when leaders are stretched thin through re-engineering, restructuring, or right-sizing. Teams can help in providing the direction and support that was once provided by a hierar-

chical structure, and in a more timely and efficient manner. And yet, team members must have experiences together if they are to really believe these benefits of teams. It is one thing to talk about accepting the diversity of the team members but quite another to embrace diversity as an asset that can help the team deal with complicated problems and challenges. By experiencing small victories as a team, people begin to believe in the personal and organizational benefits of teams. They also begin to understand the power of teams for taking on responsibility and ownership in key business decisions and their implementation. A meaningful way to facilitate this understanding is to begin breaking down the language of hierarchy. Information sharing helps to break down hierarchical thinking, and using a different language can further this process while creating empowered teams. Have people substitute "team" for "work group," "team member" for "employee," and "team leader" for "manager/supervisor." Language is a powerful mechanism for change, especially when coupled with the training and focus we have been describing regarding self-directed, empowered teams.

6. Teach team members and leaders how they can begin to hold each other accountable and recognize each other for good team member performance. The teams need to begin taking responsibility for creating and maintaining a strong team,

even though the team leader may carry more of the initial team responsibility. But it must be made clear that the long-term expectation is for all team members to share this responsibility via monitoring performance, recognizing good use of team behaviors, and correcting less-desirable behaviors. In addition, it is most useful if the organization and its senior leadership can begin to recognize teams for good performance, so people can know that the company is serious about using empowered teams. Recognition can take the form of both financial and nonfinancial rewards. The key is to begin rewarding desired team behavior both organizationally and within the teams. To fail in this tactic is to inhibit the entire movement to empowerment.

How and When Should We Begin Using Teams in the Process of Changing to Empowerment?

1. After information sharing has had time to begin building a sense of responsibility in people and has enhanced the level of trust, you will find people wanting to become more involved. By declaring the boundaries for autonomy, you provide people with guidelines for action, and by beginning to develop self-directed teams to replace the hierarchy, you will provide a vehicle people can use in taking responsible action. Hence, the time to start with teams is early in

the change process toward empowerment, but not right at the beginning. Let information sharing have a chance to build a foundation upon which the teams can operate. And do not expect miracles from the teams as they initiate action.

There are many new skills the team members and team leaders must learn. On the other hand, do expect and hold people accountable for team effort and action, even if they are small in impact. Remember, it is a good sign when the teams start asking more questions.

A Canadian bulk fuel distributor wanted to develop people into a self-directed team. In the past, the top manager's style was essentially "closed book." "Just fulfill your job description and I'll do the rest." The atmosphere this created over time was one of "Just do what you are told; don't think too much." People did not know how they made a difference, if indeed they did. Profitability was marginal at best, and morale was terrible. People merely showed up for work instead of becoming involved in it. The owner/manager realized that change would have to start with him, not them. He closed down normal operations for three days and began the empowerment process with open-book management. Every team member got to look at dollars coming in and see how much was left after expenses. At the end of the first day, one person commented, "You mean if I take one of the promo coffee cups home for a friend we have to sell 125 liters of fuel to make up the cost?" That was the genesis of a tremendous change toward an atmosphere that reflected "The only way we win is if we all win." The second day focused on an explanation of how everyone's actions affected profit. From truck driver to secretary to accountant to sales clerk, everyone began to see how he or she could make a difference. The third day focused on training that included the owner/manager, who said, "I have to be willing to look at my behavior as well." The concept of teamwork was born those three days, and after two years of continued effort, profits were up 27 percent and the atmosphere was one of "Together we can win."

2. It is possible to integrate the development of self-directed teams right into the information-sharing process, and where possible, this is desirable since we know that empowerment depends on using all three keys. Consider holding monthly information-sharing meetings and at each meeting asking a team of people to share data relevant to the work of their team. For example, a production team might share data about throughput numbers, quality measures, waste measures (including costs), value-added assessments of their work, and so forth. A customer service team might share data about the number and nature

of customer complaints, information about how the team members deal with customer complaints, tracking of recurring problems and solutions tried, and so forth. The point is to build self-directed teams through the vehicle of information sharing relative to real business issues.

One mid-Atlantic company in the packaging industry organized all its efforts at each location into teams, which were set up as individual profit centers. Each team was charged with generating a profit and with presenting its results each month at a plant meeting. The teams were given access to information to guide and inform their work. Initially, they struggled with what to do, and the expectations for the presentations were more in line with being good learning opportunities than with yielding outstanding results (though that would come further in the journey to empowerment). The results of this team focus were to draw out the talents of each member of the teams and to create a real sense of responsibility in all members of the plant organization. At first it was difficult, but gradually the teams have become true business partners to the plant management.

3. Involve teams at the information-sharing meetings in playing out "what if" scenarios that will challenge them to make team decisions about

business issues affecting the company. Pose a problem for teams to solve. For example, ask If it costs our company $100 per hour for each member of a five-person project team, how much will profits increase if we cut work input by one hour per week off a six-month project and still achieve the desired quality measures for the work? As people solve this type problem, they will begin to understand very clearly how their actions impact the business and its performance. At the same time, they will be learning how to work together—as a team—to synergistically solve real business issues. (By the way, the answer to this problem is a saving of $13,000 over the six months of this project. That is $13,000 that falls to the bottom line of the company and its profit and loss statement.) Such practice can set up the opportunity for teams to make a real impact for the company. For example, rather than have senior managers make all the budgetary decisions, the teams can be involved in modifying the budget to fit constraints. All too often, when the revenue-cost equation gets tight, the accountants decide what to do (for example, cancel all training, do not travel, and so on). Rarely do they come up with a suggestion like "Do not flush the toilets for a month to save money." The point is that such budgetary problems are ideal opportunities to involve the teams, find creative solutions to the problems, and build commitment to the solutions.

The financial group of an information services company faced some serious budgetary constraints and used teams very effectively and creatively to deal with the problem. In one of the information-sharing sessions, the teams presented a summary of the steps they followed to conduct an analysis of a particular kind of financial problem. When they finished, they noted that the process involved 237 steps from start to finish and explained that they wanted to assist in solving the budgetary problems of the company by streamlining the process without losing the appropriate checks and balances that were needed. The team members present took on the challenge and managed to reduce the number of steps from 237 to 103, which resulted in a time and cost savings of over 40 percent. In addition, the team gained valuable experience as a team and felt a real sense of pride in being able to accomplish so much.

What Are Some Ways to Help Teams Begin Making Some of the Smaller Decisions That Managers Used to Make?

1. Team training is critical to helping teams learn to make team decisions and begin dealing with

some of the smaller decisions that managers have traditionally made in hierarchical organizations. It can be beneficial to start with nonbusiness problems, which avoid the emotional element of the decision making and that are also fun. There are numerous types of decision-making problems that can be used in the training. Examples are cognitive exercises (like written survival exercises) or physical exercises (like getting team members through a maze of string without touching the string). One key element that is needed is a way to measure results so team members and team leaders can be convinced that teams can outperform individuals. A second key element is to explain team communication and decision-making practices of effective teams before the exercises and then use observers to provide feedback on how well the team members and team leader adhere to these practices. These exercises and the associated feedback are very powerful in developing the skills needed by self-directed teams, and in addition, they build the confidence of team members and team leaders to make good team business decisions on the job.

2. Team leaders should hold team meetings to share issues that must be resolved through effective team decisions and team implementation. Implementation takes the team squarely into real-world issues that can only be simulated in

classroom training. The team leader will need to provide significant guidance to the team at this early stage of development. This guidance will help a team to make decisions that are well analyzed and to which all members are committed for implementation. It will also provide the support and encouragement that team members need to work completely through a problem, even when it would be easier to let the team leader make the decision. The goal here is one of developing team skills and confidence while solving real business problems that enhance business performance.

A pollution control engineering company realized early on that it was expecting a great deal from its team leaders in the transition to teams. To help them in working through real business issues with their teams in the most constructive manner, the company held ongoing training off line for these leaders. They were taught the skills of being effective team leaders and then were expected and encouraged to use those skills with the teams they were leading. At each subsequent session with the team leaders, problem issues were discussed, new skills were developed, and a plan for implementation on the job was developed. Gradually the managers became true team leaders working with

138

> effective teams. The impact on bottom-line results has been positive and significant.

3. When teams begin making decisions that have previously been made by management, we must anticipate that they will not always make the best decisions. Of course, when a good decision is made, the team leader should be quick to praise the team for its efforts and results. And when a less-effective decision is made, the team leader must help the team view these situations as learning opportunities. It is often in the times of "failure" that teams can learn the most, but it is also important not to have team members begin pointing fingers at each other as the cause of the failure.

4. One of the important messages to get across to teams at this early stage is that they will be held accountable for making good business decisions. They cannot avoid this responsibility in a culture of empowerment. At the same time, the success of the team depends on not finding blame when mistakes are made. Team leaders must not ask, Who did it? when teams make mistakes. That is the wrong question. The right question to ask is, What went wrong and how do we fix it, as well as learn from it? By minimizing the fear of reprisal, teams can often begin rather quickly to make decisions that improve quality, reduce costs,

and increase profits. Why? Because the teams provide a vehicle for releasing the knowledge, experience, and motivation that reside within the team members. But remember, if team members hold onto the fear of reprisal for bad decisions that is so common in hierarchical organizations, their empowerment actions will be severely inhibited.

One of the questions we like to pose to people is, What is the first question that is asked when a mistake is made? If the first question is, Who did it? we know we are not in an empowered culture, and we know that movement to a culture of empowerment will be hindered. If the first question is, What was the business reason for the decision, what did we learn, and how do we ensure this mistake won't happen again? perhaps we are in an empowered culture or at least on the way there. You can just imagine what people say is the typical first question. What would it be in your organization?

5. Initially, team members may respond to empowerment efforts with a sense of "I want to make a difference" (unless they are extremely cynical of top management's ideas), but this positive euphoria is often quickly followed by an attitude of "Do I have to take on all these responsibilities?" It is vital to work with the teams to pro-

vide clarity of direction and support of their actions so that the power of the "I want to" attitude is rekindled and sustained. There is no better way to do this than to give the team clear parameters in which to make decisions, to hold the team accountable for making smaller decisions at first, and to acknowledge good work while working with the team to improve less-effective efforts. The journey to self-directed teams replacing the hierarchical mind-set can be slow, but it can gain speed when the teams begin at the right starting point.

CONCLUSION

At this point we have answers to many of the questions managers and employees (team leaders and team members) ask in this first stage of Starting and Orienting the Journey to empowerment. The process gets started with information sharing, but declaring boundaries for autonomy and developing self-directed teams (albeit with team leaders at this point) must follow quickly to provide a three-pronged effort focused on creating a culture of empowerment. Next, we will turn our attention to the second phase of the empowerment journey. We call this the stage of Change and Discouragement because it is a phase filled with difficulty and frustration, and is often a phase where team leaders and top management of a company abandon the empowerment journey. It is crucial to know how to use the three keys to get

through this tough stage of the journey to empowerment.

STAGE TWO

CHANGE AND DISCOURAGEMENT

Once the process of the change to empowerment is underway, an interesting and stressful phenomenon invariably occurs. The reality of the challenge of reaching empowerment is always more difficult than expected. Everyone underestimates just how hard it will be to change old hierarchical habits to take on the new habits of empowerment. Furthermore, people also underestimate the difficulty of changing organizational systems that have been created to support a hierarchical organization to systems that support empowerment.

In this section, we will focus on this stage of Change and Discouragement. As in the first stage, we will explore how each of the three keys to empowerment can facilitate getting through this time, when many people just want to give up and go back to where they were before. Situational Leadership® II will provide a framework for guiding us to the right use of the three keys. Focusing on the three keys will furnish us the specifics. Again, our format will be to pose questions that leaders and team members tend to have about changing to empowerment when they are discouraged and in the midst of change. We will provide answers on how to get through a period that feels like being in free fall while sky diving in clouds. The plane is only a comforting memory, and the ground is not yet in sight. (And where is that ripcord, anyway?)

First, we will focus on how to use information sharing to help people bring empowerment practices into clearer view. We will *then* explore how the other two keys play a vital role in this difficult transition stage. We will look at creating autonomy through boundaries and letting teams replace the hierarchy, in that order, all the while remembering that it takes using all three keys to get through Change and Discouragement and further down the road to empowerment. So let us first turn to the use of information sharing in this second stage of the change process.

CHAPTER 6

Key #1: Share More Information and Listen for Information

In an era of speed and quickness, we often hear people express frustration at how long change takes. Once a commitment is made to empowerment, everybody wants to reach the goal without having to make the journey. Like small children on a holiday trip, people seem to be asking, Are we there yet? The problem is that the change to empowerment from the hierarchical mind-set of the past involves the incorporation of significantly different ideas. We must, therefore, anticipate points of frustration and disappointment along the journey to empowerment. Following are some of the typical questions that can be expected at this stage of the change process.

Why Do We Have to Go through This Feeling of Discouragement?

1. It is not that feelings of discouragement are desirable during the change process; they are inevitable. In changing organizational systems, departments, and even work units, the excitement

or positive anticipation that is often felt at the beginning of the journey is followed by a realization of just how much has to change to get us to where we want to be. As Situational Leadership® II suggests, initial excitement from venturing into new territory soon turns into disillusionment or dissatisfaction, whether leaders are working one-on-one with people or with teams. An enthusiastic beginner (Development Level 1) becomes a disillusioned learner (Development Level 2), and a team at the first stage, Orientation begins to show signs of the second stage, Dissatisfaction. These are natural occurrences. Disillusionment and dissatisfaction are not bad, just uncomfortable. Moving to empowerment may sound great at the beginning, but the journey becomes difficult when people begin to understand how they (whether leaders or team members) must change both their attitudes and behaviors. As a result, people often feel bad during this important Change and Discouragement stage of the journey. One of the key issues becomes, Do we start rewarding people who demonstrate the good judgment that is needed in empowerment, or do we continue to reward compliance that is consistent with hierarchy? Most of us like change if it means the other person must change. We get a little concerned when change means we also have to make some changes.

2.   During this stage of change, many negative feelings and behavioral inhibitors for empowerment arise. People doubt themselves but often express this feeling as doubts about their leaders. To cope with these issues we must utilize information sharing in a slightly different manner than in the first stage of the journey. And we must begin to respond to the underlying questions people have about the issues they are now encountering. As the concerns model in chapter 2 suggests, people begin to have personal and implementation concerns during this second stage of the change process. They will have questions such as,

• How will I be impacted by all this change? Will I win or lose?

• Am I the only one who wonders if I will be able to make the change to empowerment? How will I find the time?

• I am not sure how this additional responsibility of empowerment will help me. What's in it for me?

• What am I supposed to do to make empowerment work? Whom can I go to for help?

• How long is it going to take to reach empowerment? When will my frustration begin to subside?

• Is this what happens in other organizations moving to empowerment, or are we having particular difficulties?

• Can't senior management make the process go more smoothly? Are they really trying to empower us, or is this just a sham?

As is apparent, many of the questions people have at this point reflect self-doubt, but as is typical, most people look for someone or some process to question rather than questioning their own abilities and/or attitudes. Also, note that the questions tend to focus on each person alone, without yet recognizing that he or she is part of a team that is developing as well. Let us look at some of the specific questions people will have and how information sharing addresses those issues, remembering, however, that the other two keys will also play critical roles.

How Do You Use Information Sharing to Help People When They Encounter Frustration and Discouragement in the Change Process?

1. One of the major reasons people will encounter frustration and discouragement in the journey to empowerment is that their initial expectations are not in line with reality. Almost everyone—from senior leadership to middle management to team leaders to team members—tends to underestimate what is involved in making the change to empowerment. Or people may have little hope the process will work, so the first sign of problems only

confirms their perception, leading to frustration and discouragement that anything can ever change the hierarchical mind-set of the past. People ask themselves whether this "empowerment thing" is ever going to fulfill its promise. Team members wonder if they will ever be freed to use their talents and judgment, while leaders wonder if the team members will ever take responsibility for results. Both team members and team leaders fear that they will appear incompetent in the culture of empowerment. Granted, they may never express this feeling openly, but it is there—slightly below the surface—just the same. It helps both leaders and team members a great deal if someone shares with them the idea that change always has this stage of discouragement. For example, if people working in teams were taught about the team development stages, they would understand that the stage of discouragement is quite natural, even if it is also quite uncomfortable. This type of information sharing gives people a big-picture understanding of what is happening, and it is best done at the time that energy starts to fall. To do it too early has little impact, since people cannot yet imagine the feelings of frustration and discouragement they will have. And to do it too late will let the situation deteriorate to a point where recovery is difficult. Dealing with issues in a "just-in-time" manner is the best approach.

One of our consulting experiences brought this point home very clearly. After we had been working with a company for about six months, there were many signs of discouragement from both leaders and team members. People were heard to say, "This empowerment stuff will never work. Our leaders don't really want us to take action on our own." At the same time, leaders were heard to say, "When will our people begin to take action? They know we want them to be empowered. What is the holdup?" It was clear that the empowerment effort was really in trouble; it was quickly becoming just another "flavor of the month" management effort. Our next step was to explain that such frustration and discouragement were not uncommon—in fact, they were to be expected in a change effort. We also explained how other companies had experienced exactly the same problems. The response was surprising; leaders and team members began to talk openly about their frustration and discouragement. Then they began to talk about how they could deal with their problems. Some said, "If those other companies could handle these problems, so can we. In fact, we can do it even better than they did."

2. It is also helpful to remind team members and leaders how they will benefit from the culture of empowerment. Tell team members that they

will benefit by having more control over their work and by feeling a sense of pride and ownership that is unlike anything they have experienced in a hierarchical setting. Reinforce for leaders that they will benefit by having people who are partners and team members and who share the responsibility for achieving results and goals. Be sure to inform people of the progress they are making both in terms of becoming empowered and in terms of the impact on bottom-line results. Even small progress should be noted since positive feedback helps to counter the feelings of frustration while also continuing to reinforce desired work behaviors and outcomes. At the same time, acknowledge that the change to empowerment is indeed a long process that, at times, will seem very frustrating and interminable.

A Midwest-based manufacturing company spent a great deal of effort at this stage preparing reports and data to share with all employees in each of its locations around the country. The data collected was of two types. First, the company used our Empowerment Barometer, which is a questionnaire designed to assess where people are along the journey to empowerment.[1] The barometer has three sections that deal with each of the three keys to empowerment. Each section has a series of statements that essentially define a state of high empowerment. When people rate their organization on each statement, it becomes clear where the gaps are between reality and the goal of empowerment. By comparing the responses of team members to those of middle managers and senior leadership, significant discrepancies come to light that may signal people are not working from the same perceptions of reality. The barometer provides a rich source of information that can form the basis of an action plan for next steps and can benchmark progress toward empowerment. In this case, the new data were compared with pre-change data to reinforce that some behavioral changes were occurring. The second type of data collected related to productivity, scrap, and quality of the manufacturing process. Again, current data were compared to prechange data to show that some bottom-line changes had begun to occur. This information sharing proved to be very helpful in combating people's frustration since it showed that positive changes were occurring in terms of both processes and outcomes.

3. At this time it is also important to focus energy on team members sharing information with the leaders. Put another way, this is the time to really hear what concerns people have. Are they worried that they do not have the skills needed to become empowered? Are they concerned that they do not have time to make all the changes that are needed to move to empowerment? Are they

frustrated that empowerment seems so far away from their present position? Just what are their concerns? An effective leader will use the principles of Situational Leadership® II to conclude that a good coaching style is best now because it involves not only continued direction but active listening, which is critical at this time. The concerns are there, but people may have a hard time articulating them clearly. Leaders will need to use active listening skills to discover the real concerns, and they must respond to these concerns with patience and empathy. Leaders should also acknowledge they are feeling many of these same concerns. By bringing these common concerns into the open, leaders and team members will be brought closer together in dealing with a common challenge, which will result in focused and enhanced energy to keep the empowerment process going.

One supermarket company enthusiastically supported the concept of more empowered team members. The leadership wanted empowerment to work, and so did the people, but nothing was changing. It became clear that measurement was the key obstacle to change. The only critical measurement in the environment was authorized store hours. So every time a store manager wanted to innovate to increase sales, there was no support from the middle managers, who were measured only on authorized hours. Of course, store hours must be measured if margins are to be managed. But the team members knew, as did the store managers, that other factors besides hours had to be valued. Only by opening up a channel of communication from team members and store leaders to middle managers could people's concerns be addressed. The result was empowered people who went beyond store hours in providing value to customers and margin to the company.

4. Managers who are learning to become team leaders will need additional training regarding how to use information sharing effectively during this stage of frustration and disappointment. Team leaders need a refined skill for sharing information about the company's performance; they need to be able to explain it clearly and also be able to respond to questions clearly and nondefensively. As the Situational Team Leadership model suggests, during the Dissatisfaction stage, team leaders, if they are going to be effective, will use a high direction/high support leadership style. They will provide direction relative to the task at hand, but they will also employ a heightened skill for listening, diagnosing, understanding team member differences, resolving conflicts, and translating problems into action plans for solution. These skills take training and practice since they are skills that are not often used in hierarchical

settings. It is also important at this time for team leaders throughout the organization to see top management modeling the desired behaviors. Without that kind of leadership and commitment from the top, any change efforts are doomed to fail.

A mid-Atlantic company conducted ongoing team skill training for its leaders, trying to teach the skills that were needed at each stage of the change-to-empowerment process. When top managers began to support this training by participating themselves, important signals were sent to all the leadership about the urgency to use these skills. By focusing early on improved communication and diagnostic skills, they were able to keep the dip of frustration and disappointment from going too low. They were especially effective in using listening as a tool for influencing behaviors in the direction desired for empowerment. The team leaders were able to use listening to discover people's true concerns and then to use listening to show people they had the skills to solve some pretty challenging problems.

What Types of Reactions Should Be Expected from Frontline People Who

Now Have Some Information but Are Feeling Discouraged?

1. During information-sharing meetings, expect some tough questions from frontline people. Remember, they feel frustrated and discouraged that this "empowerment thing" will ever work, especially to benefit them. They may express the concern that it was only to benefit the company all along—just a way to get more work out of people. The leaders of these meetings must encourage these tough questions and respond with honesty and integrity. Of course, the company hopes to get increased productivity, quality, customer responsiveness, and so forth, but the leaders and team members will gain a sense of involvement and pride that comes from being partners in these improvements.

2. Do not be surprised to have frontline people asking leaders pointed questions about the business. They may ask, "Why are margins off?" or "Why are sales increasing at a slower rate than anticipated?" or "What is being done to deal with some serious customer complaints?" These questions indicate that the people are really beginning to understand the business and that they are beginning to think like interested owners and partners. Be prepared to provide further explanation and more

information as to what various numbers mean. Also use this time to explain more about how the numbers are calculated and how they compare to the past or with industry benchmarks.

One of the most interesting meetings we ever observed was one in which a leadership team in a computer company sat in front of a group of team members responding to their questions about the business. It was clear that these people were well informed about business results, and they wanted to know why performance results of the plant were declining. They asked some very pointed questions about resources, strategic decisions, and cost containment decisions that management had made. It was clear that they felt these decisions had not been well thought through. The most amazing aspect, though, was the response of the leaders to these "attacks." They all remained very calm and responded to the team members' concerns, even acknowledging that some of the decisions had not been the best. They invited the people to offer suggestions and to work with them to develop better ways to combat the competitive pressures from the marketplace. What followed, long after the meeting, was an energy that helped the company deal effectively with many of its problems in a manner that involved employees and managers working together as team members.

3. Although it is easy for team leaders to feel pressured by people's discouragement and their thinking that the leadership should have all the answers, they should not fall into the trap of shying away from sharing sensitive information. People need to understand the real situation, be it good, bad, or mixed. By sharing sensitive information leaders will send a strong message that they respect and trust the frontline people. They will be saying, "I trust that you will be responsible with the sensitive information that I am sharing with you." They will also be asking for their people's ideas on how to have a positive impact on the numbers, especially if they indicate certain difficulties. The risk taken by sharing sensitive information at this stage of the change process will pay off because people can use their knowledge, expertise, and motivation to positively impact desired outcomes. Remember, "a company is only as sick as it is secret." Now is a time to get well and continue enhancing a culture of empowerment, and one of the key medicines in this situation is enhanced information sharing.

4. Continue the process of sharing information that lets people know how their work is impacting their departments and the company. People need to know they make a difference, that they are not just pulling a shift or wasting a day at the office. In addition to the information-sharing meetings that occur periodically, take steps to make information available whenever and in whatever form people need it. At this point they have been using the information for a while and may have ideas about additional information they need to help them perform in responsible, problem solving, and innovative ways that help bottom-line results.

5. Encourage team members to share information with each other on their teams, and praise those who do share. Information sharing is the lifeblood of empowerment and problem solving, and teams thrive on information. When team members share information with each other, they collectively learn what each person knows, thus enhancing the synergistic impact the team can have. Likewise, encourage information sharing by team members with the team leader and other levels of management. By beginning to really tap into the talent of frontline people, senior leadership can learn a great deal about how to fix organizational problems as well as gain perspective on strategic directions for the company. In addition, sharing information upward as well as downward in the organization continues the process of de-empha-

sizing the hierarchy and building a sense of partnership throughout the organization. Ask frontline people for ideas on improvement of processes and procedures and you will be surprised not only at the results, but also at the feeling of partnership that develops as empowerment is enhanced.

What Should Be Done to React to Results Achieved by People Using Their Newly Acquired Information?

1. As people enter this period of frustration and discouragement, it is critical to understand that they are likely asking themselves, Is all this effort worth it? Indeed, team leaders may be asking themselves the same question. To help people see what they are beginning to accomplish, even in this stage of frustration, they need to receive praise for their efforts as well as for actual improvements in performance and in acting empowered. Look for any improvements in areas such as new idea generation, people taking responsibility for their actions, bottom-line numbers, quality results, and so forth. Share stories of successful use of information, even if the behaviors are only approximately right. Help people to see the impact they are having, and let them know that you notice what they are doing to become empowered. Praise progress, not just end results. Set goals with trackable measures. Then, as progress is

made, do not be bashful about delivering effective praise. Too many people fail to deliver praise for progress. Others try, but they come across as too programmed, too general, and too insincere. For advice regarding cheering people on to be effective, refer to the third secret (The Gift of the Goose) in the book *Gung Ho!* by Ken Blanchard and Sheldon Bowles.[2] They contend that praising must be spontaneous and timely, individualized, specific and descriptive, and unique and sincere.

One utility company in Florida realized the need to change its performance management system to be more consistent with a culture of empowerment and partnership between leaders and team members. During initial training about the new process, data were collected from a Performance Management Barometer, which measured perceptions of the effectiveness of goal setting, coaching for performance, and reviewing performance. After about a year, when people felt some discouragement that the changes were not that significant, the barometer was administered again. The results showed significant improvement in the setting of goals and in reviewing performance. The data also identified the need for more focus on the coaching step in the process. The leadership of the company took the time to celebrate progress in a meaningful display of public praise and recognition. Everyone felt good to know that progress was being made, and all were energized to continue working together to improve the coaching partnership. In subsequent sessions, team members and their leaders alike brought up ideas for improving and solidifying a more effective performance management partnership.

In trying to use praise effectively, it can be helpful to remember the principles of effective praising from *The One Minute Manager* by Ken Blanchard and Spencer Johnson (see the chart below).[3]

EFFECTIVE PRAISING

1. Up front, clarify what is expected.
2. Describe the behavior that has occurred in specific terms that relate to expectations.
3. Deliver the description as close in time to the behavior as possible.
4. Express sincere appreciation for the good job.
5. Help the person to see and acknowledge what is good about the behavior.
6. Express confidence that you will see more of this good behavior.
REMEMBER, EVEN E-MAIL PRAISE IS
BETTER THAN NO PRAISE;
VOICE MAIL CAN BE NICE AS WELL;

FACE TO FACE IS STILL THE BEST!

Kenneth Blanchard and Spencer Johnson, *The One Minute Manager* (New York: William Morrow and Company, 1982), 44.

2. Be on the lookout for problems that are identified by the teams and solved by team effort. As they become accustomed to receiving information that has previously not been available, the fledgling teams may surprise themselves with their ability to solve important performance problems. The focus of positive feedback needs to be not only on the results achieved but also on how the team has used the information to solve its own problems in a responsible manner. Pay particular attention to how the teams use the information to track whether their solution actually fixes the problem without causing other problems. To become empowered, teams must learn to use the information that has been shared to diagnose and fix problems. At this stage of development, they need praise to let them know when they are making progress on this skill. To really enhance the team development process, also focus on how the team accomplished the solution, with particular attention to effective team effort that both achieved results and furthered the team toward being empowered.

3. One outcome is almost inevitable. Even though decisions are made with good intentions and good effort, teams will make mistakes in trying to use the information they now have available. It is critical at this time to resist the temptation to criticize people for their mistakes. Mistakes need to be viewed as excellent learning opportunities. The only people who make no mistakes during a change effort are those who take no new action. Hence, when people make mistakes using the information they have, praise their initiative and help them and others learn from their mistakes by working with them through the problem to a solution. Encourage others to share their ideas for solutions as you coach people on how to learn as a team. Work with them to generate ideas, evaluate the options, and reach a consensus as to the best solution for fixing the mistake.

4. Help employees and managers at all levels see the benefit (and the risk) from their empowerment efforts. They must see the connection between effort and benefit that comes with increased responsibility; otherwise, there will be a tendency to want to go back to a culture of hierarchy where they have less responsibility and can get by just by coming to work and doing what they are told. At this stage of the change process, the responsibility of using information to impact results will at times appear overwhelm-

ing, especially to team members. Listen to their concerns but also make clear that they are account-able for the impact of their decisions and efforts.

One company went so far as to place bells in each office of the company. When a mistake was made, someone would ring a bell to announce the mistake and simultaneously to mark the search for learning from the mistake. What the leaders tried to do was to create an atmosphere where mistakes were celebrated because they meant people were taking the risk of responsibility and innovation and because the people were providing opportunities for learning. What the leaders found was that the people did make more mistakes than in the past, but they also generated more innovative ideas, which resulted in improved performance of the work units.

What Additional Information Should Be Shared at This Stage of the Journey to Empowerment?

1. Trust between leaders and team members is still an issue at this point. While the initial information sharing may have begun to improve the trust equation, it is still fragile. At this stage of change, where frustration is felt, employees and managers alike may become cynical about empowerment.

Employees will be looking for signs that empowerment is not going to work, that management is only talking and not acting, and that this "empowerment thing" is just another passing fancy. Leaders will also be looking for signs that empowerment is not going to work, that team members will not take responsibility for actions and results, and that senior leadership will not stay the course. Indeed, team leaders will fear that senior leadership will leave them out on a limb with no support to deal with the problems of changing to empowerment. It is absolutely essential at this point in the change process to continue to share information not only about the business but also about progress on the change process. People need to know what has already happened as a result of the changes that have occurred, and they need to know what to expect from the process in the near future. Continue to entertain and respond to questions in an open and honest manner, recognizing that leaders—even senior leaders—do not always have all the answers. It is all right to say "I don't know." The only way to develop trustworthy people is to *trust!*

A change management and consulting company went through the empowerment process, and it felt many of the ups and downs we are describing here. What the leaders found though was that increased information sharing did help people get through this stage of discouragement. By providing information that could be compared to history, people began to realize just what they were accomplishing. They realized that use of the three empowerment keys in the first stage of the change had made them like their jobs better, feel more proprietary about the company, and feel more vested in creating a culture of empowerment. For example, people in the fulfillment center learned through information sharing that far fewer customers were unhappy due to delayed receipt of shipments. With a clear focus on reducing customer complaints and the encouragement to use their ideas to fix problems, they had made significant progress and felt a great sense of pride. Indeed, they wanted to tackle other problems they could see in their center.

2. At this point in the change process, you can begin to build on the kind of information that has been shared during the first stage. It will help to continue the building of trust and responsibility if you share even more sensitive information about the unit or company than has been shared up to this point. For example, share information about critical issues that are facing the company or unit in the future.

An engineering company was very bold in laying out facts that indicated the company was overstaffed and facing the possibility of layoffs. When this information was shared with team members throughout the organization, an initial fear arose, followed by an appreciation that they were being included in the decision-making process. They were being asked to consider the impact of such a decision on the company and on themselves. They were asked for ideas about how to implement the layoffs, as well as about ideas to deal with cost cuts or revenue generation that might also fix the problem. As the company has begun to emerge from this difficult time, most people feel that they have emerged much stronger and with renewed energy based upon the learning and trust building that has come from the way this situation was handled.

3. Do not be afraid to begin sharing more in-depth information about the inner workings of the company. For example, help people gain a better understanding about how pay is determined, including bonuses and incentives. Research has repeatedly shown that people perceive a bigger gap between what leadership and team members get paid than really exists. Sharing the facts helps to improve the understanding and the feelings that

go with it. People expect leaders to be paid more than team members. Besides, if you do not feel comfortable sharing the facts of the pay plan for the company, it may suggest that it is either unfair or too complex. Consider the possibility of involving people in changing the plan.

One national medical technology company had just completed a major downsizing, and the employees who were left, of course, had the "privilege" of additional work. Morale was already low, and now the people were expected to work harder. The compensation director decided to have regional forums to define the Hay System of compensation and what constitutes job grading. In essence, doing more of the same type of work one is already doing is not a reason for a raise. However, increased responsibility is. So if as a result of the downsizing someone gains budget responsibilities, direct reports, or the authority to act independently, that person will probably get a bump in job grade. The forums were a huge success primarily because leaders were perceived to care about the issue and because they wanted to involve people in the issues resulting from the downsizing.

4. Remember that sharing information is a powerful way to build trust and instill responsibility in people. At this stage of the change process, when

doubts are rising along with frustration about how long and involved the change is, enhanced information sharing can help people get out of this valley of disappointment. Take the risk of sharing more sensitive information and of asking what additional information people need to help them be empowered. A dialogue around information sharing can be extremely helpful at this point in the change process. Do not be afraid to ask, What would you like to know?

What Mechanisms Can Be Used to More Effectively Share the Right Information in a Timely Manner?

1. Information technology (IT) can be a very efficient way to share information throughout a site or company. The best information is current (not old history) and is available when people need it (on demand). What better way to provide such information than through the company network? Be sure the system is designed to allow easy access on an as-needed basis. Ask people to tell your IT department what information they feel they need and in what format they need it. Get people involved in providing input regarding accessibility.
2. Hold meetings between operations people and IT to discuss what additional information people need and in what format they need it. When the empowerment process began, some decisions were

probably made about what information to share and how to share it (for example, team meetings to allow for a two-way dialogue and for teaching how to use the information). Now it is time to ask for people's input. Ask how useful the information has been up to this point. Ask what would make it more useful in allowing them to make responsible use of their expertise, knowledge, and motivation. Ask about easy accessibility to the information. Getting people involved in these decisions will continue the trust and responsibility building and will help combat the frustration people are feeling at this time.

Can Performance Progress Be Used as a Way to Encourage People Who Are Feeling Discouraged at This Time?

1. To combat discouragement and frustration, it can be very helpful to show people how they are making a difference and making progress. Explain the results that the information indicates, and help people to see the link between their empowered efforts and these results. If you have been collecting data all along, it will be easy to assess progress on measures of key results people are impacting (for example, quality, throughput, error rates, and so on). You

can also help them see the progress they are making toward becoming empowered by using measures such as our Empowerment Barometer. A key point from *The One Minute Manager* is to praise behavior that is approximately right when you are looking for a change in behavior. When people are learning new skills, waiting for perfection can be fruitless, whereas praising progress can keep people moving and motivated to succeed with the change that is desired.

2. Show people the impact of small, incremental changes that are yielding results. Not all change must be of the momentous variety. Indeed, a series of changes that build on each other can eventually yield a bigger impact than a "big bang," one-event type of change. Besides, the encouragement that comes from positive feedback on little signs of progress helps keep people's energy up for dealing with the challenges of changing to empowerment. It's usually better to receive ten small pats on the back in a month than to receive one big celebration pat on the back at the end of the month, especially during this stage of frustration and discouragement. And if you are tracking information and looking for signs of progress, people can begin to realize positive feedback from the data itself, which only enhances their sense of responsibility.

3. Performance progress is also a reinforcer for people using the new skills they are learning in

172

the empowerment process. As their teams learn to use information and solve problems as a team, seeing the results of their efforts will help them to retain and develop these new skills. Furthermore, utilization of these new skills will lead people to become better at them, and mastery of a new skill can help reduce the discouragement that is so natural at this stage of the change process. Practice makes perfect and builds self-confidence in the change process. People will begin to find answers to the all-important questions, What's in this change for me? and Can I learn the new skills needed in a culture of empowerment?

4. Take the time to help people see that their efforts to become empowered are worth it, both to the company and to themselves. Lead them through an evaluation of the benefits that the site or company is realizing from their empowerment efforts. People want to feel that what they are doing is meaningful and impactful, so help them see what they are achieving. Likewise, they need to see the personal benefits of becoming empowered. Help people reflect on the personal satisfaction and pride that they can feel from their efforts to become empowered. At first, their frustration may block their vision. But information about how they are working together in an empowered fashion to achieve results can help to chip away at that frustration. At the same time, be open to

hearing what is still not working to create empowerment. Leaders must acknowledge that there may still be unintended obstacles to people becoming empowered, including the behaviors of the leaders themselves. Leaders need to listen to team member concerns, understand them, and then do what is needed to change and/or remove the obstacles to empowerment. Such a pattern of reacting to team members' perceived problems is another form of positive feedback to people who want to be empowered.

Should Financial Ownership Opportunities Come with Increased Involvement and Impact?

1. When people's involvement leads to positive impact, it is time to consider building ownership and bonus opportunities for them. Their feeling of ownership needs to be met with real opportunities of ownership if people are to feel truly empowered. This, of course, is a big step. It means senior leadership is giving up some of its control by being willing to share gains with team members. But it also means that people now have a real sense of responsibility, not only for the gains from progress but also for the risks of downturns in the business. As they are becoming more and more capable of impacting outcomes, they will need to see a clear link between performance and

reward (both positive and negative). The responsibility that comes with empowerment needs to be accompanied with both personal and organizational supportive mechanisms.

In a small company on the West Coast that had been going through the empowerment process and the movement away from hierarchy, discouragement was high and people wondered if all the change was worth the effort. Then they were informed of the company's improved performance and profitability due to their efforts. As a way to involve people in a meaningful use of the profit, everyone was informed that each person could decide on a unique and specific charitable gift of at least $1,000 for salaried employees and at least $500 for part timers. Each person knew that his or her efforts had resulted in this money, and now each was given the freedom to direct a contribution toward the charity of his or her choice. The positive energy and feelings of ownership and commitment to the company's empowerment efforts and to its being a good citizen made people proud to be associated with the company and made them want to accomplish even better results the next year.

CONCLUSION

We now have some ideas about how to use information sharing and related actions to help people deal with the frustration of this second stage of the change process to empowerment. This Change and Discouragement stage is natural, but it is also quite discomforting to everyone involved. And it is a time when many companies and their leadership abandon the empowerment efforts. We, of course, have two other keys that can help people get through this rough stage. So let us turn next to discuss and respond to questions about using the second key to empowerment—create autonomy through boundaries—to assist in combating the frustration of this crucial and frustrating second stage of change.

CHAPTER 7

Key #2: Widen the Boundaries to Create More Autonomy and Responsibility

Because the world of empowerment is so foreign to people in most organizations, it is easy to begin to feel lost somewhere along the journey from hierarchy to empowerment. The mileposts to progress become unclear, creating a need to reestablish the guidelines for acting in a culture of empowerment. The initial excitement about the journey becomes bogged down in the valley of discouragement. People need to be reminded where they are going and how to get there. Being lost is never a comfortable feeling. Being in free fall between the security of hierarchy and the responsibility of empowerment is even more uncomfortable. Some people in the organization will want to give up at this point, and this is precisely the time when more focus and responsibility are needed. Some of the questions people will have are along the lines of those that follow.

Why Is It So Hard to Create a Culture of Empowerment If Everyone Wants It to Happen? Why Can't We Just Get On with It?

1. As people throughout an organization or location work toward becoming empowered, it is easy for them to lose sight of the vision of what empowerment really is. They will tend to see only the problems of taking on more responsibility, losing sight of the rewards of involvement and ownership. When the going gets tough, as it always does, both managers and employees will tend to focus on all the details they must manage along with the fact that the process is not as smooth as they had expected. At this point, they need a listening ear for their concerns but also a firm and inspiring description of the land of empowerment, toward which they are headed. It is not hard to imagine journeys to climb Mount Everest where people became discouraged and lost a sense of where the top of the mountain was. Without exception, those parties that succeeded in their expeditions had leaders who were capable of keeping people focused on the top of the mountain, while allowing them the freedom and responsibility to manage the team's details to get their jobs done.

2.   Leaders and team members alike will probably begin to wonder if the discouragement they are experiencing is typical. What is interesting about this issue is that people almost always assume that their discouragement is much worse than what people in other empowerment efforts have felt. They tend to assume that someone in their situation is doing something wrong (team members assume it is the leaders, while leaders assume it is the team members) or that their situation is so unique that empowerment just may not work. They wonder if the effort is worth it, how long the journey will really take, and if the changes they are making will really be better. These doubts must be addressed if empowerment is to succeed. Indeed, it can be very helpful to explain that the frustration of being lost and not always knowing what to do next is quite normal along the journey to empowerment. We have yet to encounter even one situation where people did not fall into this valley of discouragement. Throughout the organization—from top to bottom—people must be reminded that reaching empowerment is hard work. It is not a quick fix; it means changing some deeply held beliefs about how people should act in organizational settings. Acknowledging this fact while holding up clearly the image of the empowered culture for everyone to see is critical to a successful journey.

3. Consider the following story:

In a cable television company with which we have worked, we asked the senior leadership, "Would you like to have a workforce that acts as if it owns the company and has a proprietary interest, which takes pride in its work—in short, that is empowered?" The response was a resounding *yes.* We then asked the people, "Would you like to feel pride in your job, feel as if you are making a difference, feel a sense of ownership in your contributions at work—in short, feel empowered?" Again, we got a resounding *yes.* The only problem was, it was not happening. A quick analysis of the problem pointed the finger at middle managers as resisting the change because they had the most to lose (control, power, status, and so on). We discovered, though, that the real culprit was the system and the kinds of behaviors it supported. By making the vision of empowerment clear and changing what gets measured and noticed, we found that behaviors began to change. In other words, if we had continued to measure only financial results, people would feel accountable for that alone, and behaviors would not have changed—there was too much at risk. But when the company began to measure behaviors and processes in addition to financial data, movement toward empowerment increased.

What this story emphasizes is the need to continually redirect people with words (repetition is not a bad idea in this stage) and provide measures of the vision of the empowered organization (the top of the mountain). This process was started earlier during the first stage of the empowerment journey, but it needs to continue. Perhaps even more important is the need to work with people to help them understand what empowerment means in their part of the "empowered world." What is their piece of the new vision, and how is it going to be measured? With more information available than ever before and some general sense of taking on more responsibility, many people may feel that others in the company are either far better at this "empowerment thing" than they are or that they are far worse. Either way, there is a need to help each person gain a sense of ownership for acting empowered in his or her piece of the world. Critical to this process is keeping a dialogue going between team leaders and team members. The purposes of this dialogue are to continue to clarify the empowered vision at the micro level and to ensure that the values and vision are consistent with behaviors of people throughout the organization at all levels.

4. One of the most powerful ways to define and clarify boundaries related to vision and values is through the actions of team leaders. For example, since empowerment cultures need to embrace

the value that "mistakes are learning opportunities," team leaders should be on the lookout for
mistakes that are made as people act to take
responsibility for results. When such mistakes
are made, praise people for their effort and help
them to learn from their mistakes, guilt free.
Team leaders are constantly on display for others
to assess whether their actions match the stated
values, as are members of the senior leadership.
The attitude that "mistakes are good when they
are made as people try new responsibilities" must
be lived out in everyday action. Of course, some
managers will need to be reminded when their
actions on this value and other values are incon-
sistent.

The senior leadership team of a retail company
held regular meetings focusing on boundaries and
reinforcement of the company-wide empowerment
effort. The typical agenda for the meetings was as
follows:

1. Individual reports of front-line success stories
using people's names

2. Service complaints and recovery stories

3. Stories of how team members acted responsibly on their own

4. Discussion of old hierarchical policies abol-
ished

5. Dumb things we did that perpetuate the hierarchy, such as making unilateral decisions

6. Sharing of praising stories about people using good judgment

7. Discussion of team member/team ideas acted upon by the leadership

8. Team member/team presentation of new ideas regarding cost control, quality improvement, or other relevant company needs

9. Team presentation of department profit and loss

10. Discussion of examples of decisions being made when leaders were not present

11. Sharing of stories of how you helped someone develop a new skill since the last meeting

12. Team presentation of what members are doing to develop their skills

Not all of these items were included at every meeting, but most were as an effort to keep the senior leadership focused on driving the empowerment process. A key element in these meetings was helping top management to focus on measuring factors other than financial performance, that is, on measuring the full range of actions and outcomes that are needed to reach empowerment.

Does Goal Setting Have a Place at This Stage of Changing to Empowerment?

1. At this second stage of the change to empowerment, people need to feel in control of specific actions and responsibilities. One of the real dangers to furthering the empowerment process is that people will not be able to appreciate the reality of the company (or site) vision and values. They will feel these macro images are too far removed from their daily work world and will find them useless. There is a real need for mechanisms to translate these macro concepts into more micro images that people feel they can address on a regular basis. We have found that individual and team goals are even more critical at this stage of the process than they were in the first stage. *It is important to remember that all good performance starts with clear goals.* People have more information and more experience with empowerment; what they need is more clarity for how to act autonomously in a responsible fashion. Goals provide a vehicle for this focus, especially if they are set in a collaborative manner. With more information, team members can see the need for goals that yield important results, fix problems, create innovations, or move projects along. By being

involved in the collaborative process of setting such goals, people begin to feel the real sense of ownership and responsibility that goes with empowerment.

An information services company took a rather bold step at this stage of the change-to-empowerment process. Senior leadership took the position that employees with increased information at their disposal could now identify and define some of their own goals in collaboration with their leaders. Of the five to eight performance goals that were typical for team members, the leaders instructed members to try to develop three to four of those goals themselves. At first there was some confusion, but team members quickly came to like the idea since it explicitly utilized their input and made them feel a sense of ownership. The team leaders liked it too because it helped them shoulder the burden of identifying and defining the goals that were critical to the performance of the unit. What followed was a collaborative discussion during which all of the goals were refined to be SMART, that is, Specific, Motivational, Attainable, Relevant, and Trackable.

2. Building the partnership between leaders and team members reaches a critical moment at this point in the process of transforming from managers and employees. In conjunction with goal setting, this partnership-building process can be

enhanced by also discussing the role the team leader will play in helping team members achieve their goals. When goals are set and a team member feels he or she can achieve them with little assistance, the team leader and member need to agree on a monitoring process that will allow the team leader to stay informed as the team member achieves the goal, as measured by agreed-upon standards of performance. On the other hand, if the goal is a new challenge for the team member, the leader may need to be more involved in providing direction and support for achieving the goal. The team leader will need to coach and teach the team member on how to accomplish the task, while also providing encouragement when the team member has problems. Another way of looking at this point is that the leader needs to focus on doing whatever it takes to help people accomplish their goals and learn to be fully responsible as contributors.

One interesting case in point on the issue of new types of goals and the role of the leader comes from a client that wanted to focus people's attention not only on performance goals but also on goals that related to their values. Realizing that goals are set, but values are lived, the leaders wanted to ensure that people were focused on the values of empowerment in a meaningful way. For example, if a value is "better relationships between departments," people might set a goal around the question What am I going to do this year to improve the relationships between my department and others? Or if a value is for people to "grow in skills and abilities," a goal might be, based on the question What new skill am I going to learn this year, and how will I demonstrate the new skill? The leaders found that this gave people tremendous clarity and accountability about values and performance goals. When coupled with an expectation that leaders will do whatever it takes to help people achieve their goals, the leaders learned an attitude of serving team members with an intention of ensuring winning and growth for everyone.

3. By listening to team members' ideas and using as many as possible, team leaders can create a process whereby team members learn to evaluate data and problems and to set goals for themselves and for their teams. Such dialogue helps people to see clearly that the leadership sincerely wants their input on decisions that affect performance and that solve problems with products, services, and quality. It also goes a long way toward identifying potential goals that may have been overlooked by the leadership.

In one manufacturing company, leaders opened up such a dialogue and were amazed to find how many important concerns were identified by people that had gone unnoticed by the leaders. Many of the issues that people identified were of small impact on bottom-line results, quality, or customer service, but they had a huge combined impact that pleased both team leaders and top management. The impact also confirmed to the team members that their experience and ideas were valued by the leadership and useful to company performance. The U.S. Quality Institute found that processes like this increased the number of suggestions for improvement per person from .21 per year to over 25 per year, with a return on investment of over 4,000 percent. Indeed, involving people in the goal-setting tasks of a company pays big dividends.

4. Involving people not just in accomplishing goals but actually in setting goals to improve company or site performance is a very powerful mechanism for confirming the vital role people play in an empowered culture. Asking for and using team member input confirms for leaders that team members have valuable ideas and that they want to be responsible for organizational performance. Likewise, it will confirm for people that team leaders value

and will use their ideas, thus including them as partners in a process of improving company indicators of successful performance.

Should We Use Team Goals to Reinforce the Team Effort of Empowerment?

1. Team goals are an important device because they engage team members and team leaders in a dialogue that not only establishes clear goals but also helps to build the team as a unit. Most people have had far more experience with individual goals that were either set by their manager or, in enlightened cases, set in a communication between leader and team member, than with team goals. Hierarchies tend to be built around individual responsibility, whereas empowered cultures are built around team efforts. At this stage of the change-to-empowerment process, it will be important to create a mix of individual and team goals in order to build from the past experience of people toward the empowered culture. Over time, a shift can be made toward a greater percentage of team goals, including team-based measures of performance. Effective team goals should meet the same criteria as effective individual goals. As discussed in chapter 4, goals to be effective should be SMART (Specific, Motivational, Attainable, Relevant, and Trackable) and answer

the five questions related to this acronym. The conversation that a team has with the team leader around these five elements of a SMART goal can build a very *motivational* boundary for autonomous action of the team. In particular, discussions around the *specific* measures and how they will be *trackable* help the team use the information that has been shared. The discussion about whether or not the goal is *attainable* can help teams establish "stretch" goals that will allow the team to achieve far more than a collection of individuals could achieve, while the conversations about how these goals are *relevant* to site or company goals helps the team clarify the big picture in which they play such an important role.

2. By asking team members to focus on their team's performance (on both financial and nonfinancial, process areas) and determine where performance improvement goals should be set, team leaders gain valuable insight from many sets of eyes, rather than just their own. Just as teams of people can accomplish more than individuals, teams can assess data, define problems or opportunities, and make plans for improvement that will astound individuals—especially leaders. It is important, however, to recognize that at this stage of the change-to-empowerment process, teams still need help in setting and accomplishing goals. The discouragement they will be feeling may override their power to perform unless team (and individ-

ual) goals can be collaboratively set to define and clarify their boundaries for autonomy and unless they can receive encouragement to use their talents to achieve those goals. A useful framework for engaging the team in this process of establishing a structure for their autonomy is shown below and described by Ken Blanchard and Robert Lorber in their book, *Putting the One Minute Manager to Work.*[1] To improve performance, they contend that leaders and team members must pay the PRICE (Pinpoint, Record, Involve, Coach, and Evaluate)—a five-step process to improve performance by setting in place clear directions and measures and by developing a plan of action to which team members are committed.

Using this model can provide needed structure for the teams while creating a sense of ownership for performance improvement. Combined with Situational Leadership® II, the PRICE process can be an excellent vehicle for partnering for performance. The *pinpoint, record,* and *involve* steps help establish the goals and appropriate leadership style. The *coach* step is where the agreed-upon leadership style is delivered. And finally, the *evaluate* step ensures that timely feedback can be given and received, setting up a new cycle of PRICE.

3. Help teams and their leaders use information that has been shared—and is being shared—more regularly to define areas for continuous, ongoing

improvement. By focusing on continuous improvement, rather than momentous improvements, teams and their leaders will experience a feeling of progress toward getting results and feeling empowered. As we have said before, information is the lifeblood of an empowered organization. Helping teams learn to use it effectively to establish goals, assess progress, and measure success will build their skill and confidence to act responsibly as empowered teams.

THE PRICE PROCESS

4.   Teams can focus not only on setting performance goals but also on skill development and career enhancement goals. By having the teams focus on what actions must be taken to improve performance, team leaders can help the teams identify skills that must be developed both for the team as a whole and for its individual members. We typically find that teams must learn to work together effectively, meaning they must learn to make consensus decisions, resolve conflicts, and listen effectively in a team setting, among other key team skills. Clarification of these skill development goals will help the team take responsibility for its ability to work as a team. It will also support the idea that the organization is concerned with empowerment in the long run—that is, this "empowerment thing" is to be taken seriously and the culture will be changing. In addition

192

to this long-term concept, certain skills that individuals learn in the team context may be useful in their achievement of career aspirations. Each person on the team becomes a "work in progress" as they define career goals that support the long-term efforts of the team and the company. Such boundaries begin to create a real feeling of being in control, which is a key feeling for the culture of empowerment.

THE PRICE PROCESS

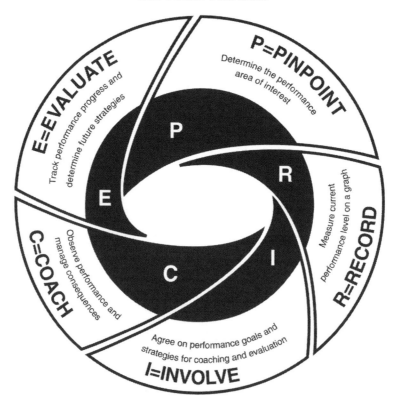

Kenneth Blanchard and Robert Lorber, Putting the One Manager to Work (New York: William Morrow and Company, 1984), 84.

In a small manufacturing company, initial efforts to involve teams in setting performance improvement goals resulted in very few suggestions. But the team leaders maintained the effort and acknowledged each and every suggestion for improvement. Gradually, with training and clear expectations that people would become involved, the number of suggestions began to increase. In just two years, the number of ideas rose to over five per year per employee with better than 60 percent implemented (the national average for suggestions per employee per year is approximately .21 with only 10 percent implemented). And some of the suggestions were significant in their impact. For example, one suggestion regarding salvage of parts resulted in savings of over $100,000 in a little over twelve weeks. In addition, a sense of team ownership was expressed in the comments of team members who were heard to say, "It doesn't matter what name is on the gate—this is my company."

What Changes Will Be Needed in the Company Performance Management System?

1. At this stage of the change-to-empowerment process, people will very likely notice and point

out inconsistencies between the company performance management system and the values of an empowered culture. First of all, most company systems are really not systems; they are simply once-a-year mad rushes to complete a form on everyone in the company. Some hard questions must be asked about the "system" the company is using. How do people, both leaders and team members, feel about the process? How many like it? How many believe it is fair? How many dread it? Is the process punitive or developmental? Is it a partnership process between leaders and team members? Most companies with which we have worked had negative answers to these questions. How could people like a process that is based on the completion of a form using limited information dominated by the most recent events over the past year? How could they feel it is fair if they had never established clear goals and performance measures at the beginning of the cycle? Typically, the performance appraisal form that may have sufficed in a hierarchy is found severely deficient in a culture of empowerment. The process has to be significantly revamped.

A humorous example that Ken has used for years relates back to his days teaching in college. Most faculty members seem to guard their final exams like they were the gold in Fort Knox. Ken, on the other hand, would give out his final exam the first day of class. His colleagues thought he was crazy. His response was, "I thought we were supposed to teach these kids, so not only am I giving them the exam up front, but I'm going to teach them the answers on the exam. I want all my students to get As, don't you?" His colleagues just shook their heads in disbelief. For us, performance management should be about getting As. As leaders, we should want all our people to succeed. Performance planning should be like giving out the final exam on the first day. Ongoing coaching is like teaching and helping people to succeed. And performance evaluation is like giving an exam for which everyone is prepared.

2. It is critical to the success of the empowerment effort to revise the company performance management system so that it utilizes and reinforces effective goal setting. With a system that uses SMART goals to initiate the performance process, team members will not have to guess what is really important to accomplish during the performance cycle. It almost goes without saying that people with unclear goals are destined to waste time and effort, resulting in inefficiency and, even worse, resulting in the inhibition of the partnership between team members and the team leader that is needed in a culture of empowerment. Even though goals were initiated during the first stage of the change-to-empowerment process, they

must be reinforced in this stage and linked clearly to the important organizational system of performance feedback and review. In addition to collaboratively setting goals for a team member to achieve, team members and team leaders need also to agree up front about the appropriate leadership style that the team leader should use for each goal that the team members will be pursuing. By so doing, the teams are set up to have the right degree and type of coaching needed to achieve each goal. Furthermore, the process establishes a partnership between team members and the team leader. We strongly recommend that performance be measured in terms of a broad set of goals. Do not place all the emphasis on financial measures of success if you expect to shape behaviors for teamwork in an empowered culture. Consider other measures for team members such as the number of team recoveries from service complaints, the number of times the team solved a problem without the help of the team leader, and the impact of team members' suggestions for improvement. For team leaders, consider measures such as development actions provided for team members, the number of times the leader got the team involved in problem solving situations, follow-through with the agreed-upon leadership style, and what the leader has done to help people succeed in goal accomplishment.

Several of our clients have undertaken to revise their performance appraisal processes—or perhaps we should say to "remake" their process—into a performance management process. They realize that their appraisal form and how it has been used are not very empowering. A typical flow to the revision effort has been to define three critical steps to a successful process:

1. Planning, which involves goal setting for the team member and agreeing on leadership style for the leader

2. Coaching, which includes effective monitoring, listening, feedback, and problem solving focused on goal accomplishment

3. Reviewing, which focuses on both the team member's performance relative to the goals and the leader's performance regarding the leadership style

Training of both leaders and team members is also essential to the change, along with a method for monitoring how the system is working and changes that must be made. The form that is used is the last element to be developed, but it is a form that supports each of the three steps in the process and that helps make it a collaborative process between team members and leaders. Companies that have made the effort to create such an empowering system have reaped many benefits, not the least of which is increased performance.[2]

3. Many company systems, structures, and proce-
    dures that are related to the performance man-
    agement process will need to be assessed, and
    many will need to be changed to create a struc-
    tural world that supports empowerment. At this
    stage of the change process, it is important to
    listen to the concerns of the people. They often
    feel caught in a quandary. Many of the structural
    constraints that existed in the old hierarchical
    culture must be altered, but when they are, peo-
    ple typically have mixed reactions. They wonder
    what to do and how to do it now; they feel a
    sense of loss for structure (even though they did
    not like many of the old structural constraints, at
    least they knew how the game was played). They
    want guidance but they also see old procedures
    and policies as inappropriate for empowerment.
    They wonder what to ask for and are sometimes
    afraid they may get it.

An international medical technology company
encountered an interesting situation when trying to
entice district managers to engage in more planning
for their installation projects for clients. It was clear
that much time was being wasted. Most projects
went over timelines and therefore had lower than
expected profit margins. During training on how to
better plan and manage projects, it became clear
that there was a structural constraint that was going

to limit the implementation of the new ideas. In calculating the bonuses of the district managers, planning time above a certain amount resulted in a decrease in bonuses. What rational person would knowingly do something to lower his or her bonus? The solution was to alter the bonus formula so that planning time was rewarded. The impact on project timelines and profit margins was significant once this structural change was instituted.

4. Begin to think about creating a pay system that rewards team members like business owners. One of the goals of empowerment is to enhance site and company performance, as measured on the bottom line. If people throughout the company take on more responsibility and the results are positive, the initial sense of satisfaction and contribution will be a significant reward to people. Eventually, however, and probably beginning during this second stage of change, people will begin to wonder about financial rewards for helping so directly to improve company performance. A system that treats people like owners will tie both rewards and risks directly to performance. When the site or company does well, team members will benefit through bonuses and stock options (where available), but when company performance is poor, team members will share the risk with senior management. An additional

step would be to get the team involved in distributing bonuses when warranted by company performance. These suggestions would begin to change the philosophy from paying for time to paying for performance.

One manufacturing company adopted a model drawn from the World Series of baseball. Many major-league teams have a system for voting on the number of World Series or playoff game shares a player should receive from the pool given to the team for appearing in or winning a series. In this company, senior management developed a system for giving the teams a pool of money based on company, division, and team contribution. But the teams decided how to divide up the money among their members. At first, they just gave everybody equal shares. However, those who had carried more of the load felt cheated. After some discussion, they began to differentiate among the team members based on individual contribution. When this led to a feeling of competition, they finally moved to define clear contributions expected of each member and when each member delivered—which is exactly what happened—there was equal distribution of a now larger bonus to the team.

5. A very significant change to most performance management systems will be in the focus of the

system. In most organizations, performance appraisals are based on the performance of individuals. In moving to a culture of empowerment, the focus needs to shift to being based, at least in part, on team performance. Put directly, if we expect team performance while rewarding only individual performance, we will not get the kind of team performance that is desired. Team members will feel a sense of competition that is disruptive to the team. *To get good teamwork, expect it, measure it, and reward it.* Then let the teams assess the performance of their individual members.

What Changes Should Be Made Now in the Type and Scope of Decisions People Can Make?

1. In dealing with the discouragement that people feel in this stage of changing to empowerment, it can be very effective to expand the range of decisions that people can make. Such expansion will send a clear signal of support and encouragement throughout the organization. When people feel their ideas count and they have responsibilities for significant decisions, they feel valued, which decreases their discouragement. The types of decisions that people can make at this stage of the change process should be larger in scope than those encouraged during the first stage. As

pointed out during the discussion of boundaries to create autonomy during that first stage (chapter 4), our Australian colleague, Trevor Keighley, has developed a very useful tool for this discussion, called the Self Direction Assessment (SDA).[3] This instrument suggests types of decisions that are increasingly more complex and thus acts as a guide to moving to deeper and wider boundaries for team decision making.

In the early stages of movement to empowerment, teams should be allowed to make decisions that are not too complex. From the PTD Group in Australia, Trevor Keighley's SDA suggests decisions such as "maintaining housekeeping and safety," "internal customer contact," and "measuring quality" can be made in the early stages of moving to empowerment. During this second stage of change, decisions such as "determining training needs," "production scheduling and control," and "managing suppliers" can be made. Each organizational situation will be unique, thus the suggestions from the SDA are just guidelines to stimulate your thinking.

---

2. In enlarging the scope of decisions that people are expected to make, it can be helpful to consider restructuring the company into business profit centers. Such centers will still have specialized tasks, but they will also have accountability for

business results. The key idea in such restructuring is to help people think as business-people who manage results. By enlarging the decision making to include managerial decisions, not just more decisions at the same level of responsibility, team members will learn how to act as owners of the business. They will understand how to be accountable for revenue, costs, and profitability, as well as for completing their tasks.

3. Continue to reinforce that teams and their members are accountable for results. Hold people accountable for identifying problems and fixing them, and expect them to draw on information that has been shared to measure problems and their solutions and on their own expertise to fix the problems. When performance problems occur, team leaders should not automatically step in to fix the problems. They need to work with the team members to improve the situation using the team members' skills, knowledge, and motivation. Team leaders must continually be on the lookout for empowerment efforts and for improved results, and they will want to be sure to recognize and praise such efforts and results in order to reinforce the actions and outcomes that are desired in the empowered culture. Although accountability for results means that team members are responsible for results, team leaders are responsible for guiding change toward the vision of an empowered organization. Team member responsibility

for results without team leader responsibility for guiding and shaping behavior will result in the empowerment effort becoming bogged down in this stage of discouragement. On the other hand, when the two accountabilities work in tandem, real progress toward empowerment can be made.

4. Work with people to draw out their ideas regarding old policies and procedures that may be inhibiting the empowerment efforts of team members. Many policies and procedures that made sense in a hierarchy will not make sense in a culture of empowerment. Ask people what is getting in the way of their acting empowered, making key decisions, and acting responsibly. Examples might include sign-off procedures before action can be taken, corporate policies that describe in great detail what people cannot do or from whom they must get permission to act, and voluminous policy manuals that seem to cover every possible scenario. Such residuals from the old hierarchical culture tend to squelch the initiative of people who want to be empowered and tend to reinforce the feelings of those who continue to doubt the sincerity of the senior leadership for empowerment. The dilemma is that leaders cannot even imagine the consequence of all these policies and procedures. Hence, opening the door for input from team members not only brings the problems to the surface but also gets people involved in taking ownership in the process. By re-

moving the barriers, team leaders and senior management are also removing the excuses for team members not to take action and responsibility and furthers the empowerment process.

5.   Another element to look out for and get feedback on is how policies are interpreted and reinforced in ways that block empowerment. Team members should be encouraged to let management know where policies are being interpreted in "dumb" ways. Leadership must then take action to change the policy or how it is being used.

An experience that John had provides a good example of this issue. He went into a retail store to buy some batteries, which cost about $2.79. When he went to check out, the clerk asked John if he could have his name. John said, "Okay, it's John Carlos." Next, the clerk asked for his address. At this point John said, "I don't need to be on your mailing list. I just want some batteries." The clerk responded, "I can't sell you the batteries unless you give me this information." John said, "Forget the batteries. I'd like to buy that $4,800 computer over there." He got the same response from the clerk—no information, no sale. John then said, "Let me get this straight. You're not going to take my $4,800 unless I give you this information first." The clerk replied, "That's right. It's our policy." Later we learned that the marketing department had initially requested the information be collected *if possible without inconveniencing the customers.* But then someone wanted more information and set up a competition to see which store could get the most names and addresses. The store managers responded by insisting the team members get names and addresses. No doubt some clerk in some store opened up the phone book and began entering names and addresses just to keep the store managers happy. A good idea was converted into a poorly implemented policy. In such cases, team members are in the best place to identify what has gone wrong, so listen carefully.

CONCLUSION

The valley of discouragement is a difficult stage of the journey to empowerment. It is somewhat paradoxical that giving people more responsibility—by widening and deepening the boundaries—is the antidote for this discouragement. It works because it directly addresses the underlying concern that the team members cannot or will not become empowered and that leaders are not sincere or are afraid of the thought of people becoming empowered. The boundaries of the empowered culture will challenge and inspire people to keep moving toward empowerment, but to succeed they must also be aided by the empowered teams that are continuing to develop. Let

207

us turn now to the third key for empowerment to see how replacing the hierarchy with self-directed teams works with boundaries and information to help get people through the valley of discouragement.

CHAPTER 8

Key #3: Let Teams Take on More of the Hierarchical Roles

During the discouragement stage of changing to empowerment, people may feel very alone, seemingly unaware that others all around them are experiencing the same concerns. Some of the issues and questions that will be going through their minds are as follows:

1. I wonder if others feel as awkward and strange about these changes as I do.
2. I used to know what was happening and how to do my job. Now I feel lost and unsure about how to do my work.
3. I'm not sure I have the skills that are going to be needed in a culture of empowerment.
4. How much of this change effort can I handle now? When will it stop, anyway?
5. Some people seem so ready to change, but I'm not ready yet. Or, just the opposite, I'm ready to change but everybody else seems to be dragging their feet.
6. Is this all rhetoric, or will I actually be rewarded for taking initiative and using good judgment?

7. Will the measurements ever change to support the authority of the team?

It is interesting to note that everyone experiences many of these same feelings, although each person thinks he or she is alone in the disillusionment. Unfortunately, the voices that tend to be heard most often during this stage are the voices of those with negative attitudes about the change to empowerment. The valley of discouragement is deep and the sides of the valley are steep. Sometimes it is hard to see how to get out, and this uncertainty applies to both team members and leaders. The solution lies with the team members and leaders, but in changing to empowerment people tend to have many questions about how teams can help.

What Role Can Teams Play at this Stage of the Change-to-Empowerment Process?

1. On the surface, this question is a difficult one to answer. Self-directed teams are not yet fully developed or empowered. They are not yet functioning at full capacity, and they are not yet making the more complex decisions. One key distinction between teams and self-directed teams is the ownership and pride self-directed teams feel in making important decisions. But they also feel the pressures that traditionally were felt by leaders. Hence, at this stage of

discouragement, the teams have not developed the needed skills of a team and they are discouraged.

As Situational Leadership® II and the Situational Team Leadership model from chapter 2 explain, the teams continue to need guidance and direction from the team leader about what to do and how to do it. They also need support from the team leader. But it is important to note that one advantage of teams as they develop is that their members can begin to support and encourage each other as they all work through the valley of discouragement. The team leader has to play a critical role by demonstrating how to provide support and direction to the team members. By so doing, he or she will begin to elicit the same kinds of behaviors from the team members themselves. The diversity of the team means that each team member may potentially have information or insight that is unique within the team. Thus, when a related issue arises, that team member can step forward and exercise some direction for the rest of the team. Likewise, different team members will feel frustration at different times. Those feeling less frustration can step forward and provide support to help the other team members get through the tough times.

In one company in the information services industry, the teams made a conscious effort to identify the talents of each team member. They called it a team assets inventory, and the result was made public to all team members. Then when issues arose that related to a particular expertise, the appropriate person was encouraged by the team leader to take a leadership role in working on that issue. The team members were reluctant to use their talents until others on the team began to add their words of encouragement. With the stage set for sharing leadership, more and more team members began to recognize when they could make a contribution and began to step forward, sometimes with ideas or suggestions and at other times simply with words of encouragement and praise for others.

2. Team leaders can really help teams combat discouragement by expecting them to play an ever-increasing role in getting the job done. It is important, however, for team leaders not to "abandon ship" and turn everything over to the teams at this stage of the process. The teams are not ready for this full responsibility yet, and to expect it of them is to court disaster and regression away from empowerment. But it can be almost as bad not to expect more from the teams at this stage than during the first stage of the change-to-empowerment process. They still have much to learn, but by expecting more from them at this point in time, it becomes clear what they have learned. They feel a real sense of pride in being

given more responsibility to think and act. The trick, if there really is one, is to find a range of moderation where the teams feel challenged but not overwhelmed. Two good ways to monitor their reaction are to talk with them about their expectations and to observe and discuss with the teams the outcomes of their work.

Our colleagues Eunice Parisi-Carew and Don Carew encourage discouraged teams to keep moving forward by conducting additional work on the very powerful focusing technique—called Team Chartering—which we referenced in chapter 5.[1] By continuing to use this technique, the team members stay engaged under the leadership of the team leader in clarifying and "signing up" for a number of key issues. By sorting out these issues, the team can feel a sense of focus and accomplishment that will help with the discouragement of this stage of the change process. The complex and extensive chartering process helps the team reach agreement on eight key areas: (1) organizational vision, purpose, and values; (2) team vision, purpose, and values; (3) norms and ground rules; (4) roles; (5) key responsibility areas and goals; (6) communication strategies; (7) decision making, authority, and accountability; and (8) resources. As the teams work through these points, they resolve how to work together and feel a sense of team accomplishment,

both of which help with their feelings of discouragement.

3.   Be sure that teams are using the skills they already have. They may be good at communicating
with each other or problem solving or any of a
variety of other team skills. The point is to find
out what they can do well together and to hold
them accountable for using those skills. At the
same time, be sure to provide the teams with
skill training where there are deficiencies. For
example, teams often need enhanced skill training
in consensus decision making, conflict resolution,
listening, and praising. Find out what team skills
are lacking and work to build those skills among
the team members. It is also very helpful to be
sure the teams understand that the disillusionment they are experiencing is quite normal. Indeed, it is a necessary stage for the development
of an empowered team.

A financial services group engaged us in a year-
long training effort to impart skill training to their
teams in a just-in-time manner. They were constantly addressing team skill needs and designing training
to teach those skills. The teams then were regularly
trying to use the new skills and let us know where
they were having problems. By the end of the year,

the teams had become quite good at team communications, consensus decision making, conflict resolution, supporting each other, and sharing leadership. Their results reflected the application of these skills through demonstrated performance improvements using a variety of measures.

In another organization in the retail food industry, the teams agreed on a specific course of action to follow when conflict arose. First, they would discuss how each member of the team felt about the issue and why. Second, they would discuss what would have to change for each team member to feel comfortable. Third, they would focus on what they were willing to do as individuals to reach a comfort zone. Fourth, they would discuss what support they needed from management. And last, they would identify any policies that were preventing empowerment or resolution.

What Types of Responsibilities Can Teams Be Expected to Take on at This Time?

1. At this time of discouragement, teams will need to experience some successes. By doing so not only will they feel better about their team, but they will

also see that they are contributing to the success of the site or company. The key here is to be sure the teams tackle some challenging problems but that they have a reasonable chance of success. A useful way to identify the problems is for the team leader, who still must play a leadership role, to engage team members in a problem identification discussion based on the information the team has available. Such a discussion will ensure that the team sees it is using the information available to it. With the leader present to provide guidance, the team will be more likely to identify challenging but solvable problems.

2. Teams will be feeling discouraged at this stage of the change process. They need experienced managers who support the values of empowerment to serve the teams as team leaders. The main role of the team leaders at this time is to continue to provide the direction that the teams cannot yet provide for themselves and to provide the encouragement for team members to step forward and exercise some leadership themselves. This is a delicate time in the change process. Team members will be reluctant to take too many risks, and they will also doubt the ability and commitment of leaders to help them through this tough stage. Team leaders must continue to show the team how to become self-directed through coaching and support. But a key point to note is that the team leaders, even though they are experienced managers who value empowerment, will also encounter times when they are unsure of what to do

next or will even doubt that the whole empowerment effort will work. At this time, the teams will often help the leaders get through this valley of discouragement, as they all are learning to work together in a culture of empowerment.

In an engineering design company, the teams started off with a great deal of excitement and desire to get involved. They offered many suggestions and tried to sort them out to make decisions, but they were unable to make effective team decisions on many problems. The teams fell into a period of frustration and began to complain that they did not know what to do. They blamed their team leaders for all the difficulties they were having. Their leaders were also confused as to what to do, which left the teams to receive most of their guidance and support from ongoing team training. Gradually, the training was internalized. The team members felt more comfortable exercising leadership, and the team leaders felt more comfortable acting as team members who exercise leadership as appropriate to their expertise. At the end of about a year, the teams were showing signs of functioning as empowered teams. They tackled important company problems, made decisions about solutions, and implemented their ideas. Improvements were noted in several measures important to company performance.

3. This is an opportune time for the team leaders to draw ideas out of the teams—ideas about how to improve performance, provide better customer satisfaction, reduce costs, and so forth. The responsibility to identify opportunities for improvement eventually needs to reside largely in the self-directed teams, and this is the time to begin to expect teams to use their experience and knowledge to this end. The results of this effort will often surprise the team leaders and even the team members themselves. Both leaders and members of the teams will experience firsthand the power of the teams to identify and solve real company problems. They will be experiencing the value of empowerment on a small scale, thus helping everyone to climb out of the valley of discouragement.

4. During the first stage of the change-to-empowerment process, the teams started to take on some simple decisions. In this second stage, it will be helpful to draw upon the teams' decision-making skills that have been previously taught and to give the teams greater decision-making responsibility. By allowing them to make more complex decisions that previously were restricted to leaders, the teams will solidify their skills and be encouraged by seeing their abilities in action. Examples of such decisions come from the work of our Australian colleague, Trevor Keighley, and include, for example, stopping work to deal with quality concerns, determining how to respond to customer complaints, and cross-training of team members.[2] The idea is to identify decisions

and tasks that involve increased complexity, difficulty, and consequences. The teams are better able to handle these more demanding tasks and decisions, but it is important not to jump too far ahead by asking them to tackle problems where the risk of failure is too great. Obviously, this situation involves judgment, which is why the team leader must stay involved in the team discussions and in monitoring their progress. The Self Direction Assessment model and process from Trevor Keighley provides useful detail for guiding the team toward becoming self-directed (see diagram below).

Each of the four levels in the model relate to giving the teams increased decision-making authority. The area under the downward sloping diagonal line provides a relative understanding of the amount of decision making authority the team leader exercises—it decreases as you move from Level One to Level Four. (Please note that the chart flows from right to left.) The area above the line relates to the decision-making authority of the team—it increases as you move from Level One to Level Four. Level One is clearly when the culture is one of hierarchy or perhaps during the beginning stage of changing to empowerment. Levels Two and Three increase the amount of decision-making authority for the team, and Keighley's materials provide great detail on the types of decisions that are appropriate for each level of development. Level Four relates to a team

---

nearing the stage of self-direction and empowerment.

The Self-Direction Assessment Model for Teams

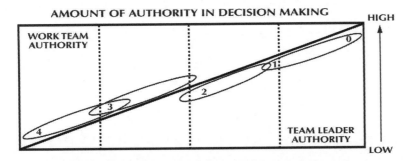

STAGES OF AUTHORITY IN DECISION MAKING

4 3.5	3 2.5	2 1.5	1 0.5 0
LEVEL FOUR	**LEVEL THREE**	**LEVEL TWO**	**LEVEL ONE**
Complete Authority	Limited Authority	Very Limited Authority	No Authority
The team makes decisions and takes action within clear boundaries without consulting leaders and management beforehand.	Authority is limited to the extent that the team must involve leaders and management in any decisions made and discuss actions to be taken (before they are taken).	The team is consulted before leaders and management make decisions or take any action.	The team can't make decisions or take action on the task.
3.5 When the team has begun making decisions on its own. The scope of the decision may at first be different (e.g. shorter timeframes, smaller budget.)		**1.5** If the people are sometimes asked for their opinions, ideas, and feelings before decisions are made by management.	**0** If the people are uninformed about the task (i.e., they have no information about it).
	2.5 If people have started to make decisions about a task or responsibility, with management involved in discussions.		**0.5** If the people are at least partly informed about the task.
4 When the team is reporting actions taken and decisions made within normal managerial budget, timeframes, etc. for such responsibilities.	**3** If decisions are capable of being made with little input of management time or information.	**2** If the people are always consulted fully about any decisions or actions being taken, and the decision is made by management.	**1** If they are well informed about all decisions and actions being taken about the task.

LEVEL ONE (on the right) represents teams in a hierarchy.
LEVEL TWO represents the beginning of empowerment.
LEVEL THREE represents team decision making during the second stage of changing to empowerment.
LEVEL FOUR represents a fully empowered, self-directed team.

Developed by Trevor Keighley ©PTD Development Trust, 1996

From Trevor Keighley, Empowering for Performance (Sydney, Australia: PTD Development Trust, 1996), 18.

5. Anticipate stalls in the change process. Teams may not always be ready to take on the responsibility for decisions as quickly as the leadership would like, but the reverse can also be true. Sometimes the teams will want to take on responsibilities that the

leadership—especially the team leaders—is not yet ready to give up. The transition of decision making and problem solving will be anything but smooth since team members and team leaders may move at different rates of speed and sometimes in different directions. Because of these varied factors, it is essential that team members and team leaders keep a dialogue open and ongoing. Information must flow in both directions to help smooth out the dips and turns in the process of transferring responsibility from leaders to team members as the organization moves toward a culture of empowerment.

6. Remember, a primary cause of disillusionment may be that the teams do not believe that accountabilities have changed, as was promised. Company leadership has to be willing to change what it measures to include team-level outcomes and processes, as well as the development of team skills of the members. The new measurements must include consequence management just like financial and production measures do; otherwise, they will not be viewed as important in the full scheme of activities of the company or site. In addition, company leadership must hold itself and middle management accountable for "walking the talk" of empowerment. Such accountability is critical for helping the teams move past discouragement and for speeding up the process of changing to empowerment.

What Systems Changes Can Support Teams and, at the Same Time, Hold Them Accountable for Results?

1. When the process of moving to empowerment began, people were informed that responsibility would be shifting from leaders to empowered teams. At this point in the process of change, it is helpful to remind and clarify that the teams are being held accountable for successfully accomplishing site and company goals as well as how they accomplish them. Empowerment is not just a culture of involving people in the company. It is also a culture of holding people much more accountable for bottom-line results as well as the actions and development of people than is ever the case in a hierarchical culture, where managers primarily carry this burden and employees tend to do what they are told. By setting team goals that tie directly to company and site goals, teams can be held accountable for contributing to company performance. However, it is important at this stage of the change to empowerment for the team leaders to coach the teams so they learn how to be successful. That means celebrating their successes (even their approximate successes) and showing them how to correct mistakes and perform more effectively.

In a company in the food processing industry, many of the systems were changed over time to put more responsibility on the teams. After several years of working on team skills and gradually shifting responsibilities, the teams essentially performed the responsibilities normally assigned to managers. They made hiring and firing decisions, handled members' performance reviews, scheduled work, handled the budget, and solved most of the critical problems they encountered. They truly became self-managed, and the bottom-line results have been outstanding. Along this journey, though, there were many pitfalls. The leaders had to help correct mistakes and teach the teams how to avoid them in the future. And the leaders had to help the teams celebrate successes, to reinforce aspects that were going well, and to keep up the energy for change on the teams.

2. At this point in the process, it is time to begin making significant changes in the performance management system of the company. The three-step model described in one of the examples in chapter 7 (planning, coaching, and reviewing) can guide the development of a new system that is empowering, but teams must be integrated into the process in a clear and definable way. Team-based goals need to become more and more common in the organization. Begin using team-based evaluations and rewards as part of the re-

view step of the performance management system. Be sure that the evaluation/review step of the process is a validation of what has been occurring throughout the performance cycle. The teams should not be receiving new information at the time of the review. Now, all this is not to say that individual goals and evaluations are not to be used, but a greater emphasis needs to be on team goals and evaluations if we expect teams to become empowered. What good is accomplished if an individual succeeds and the team fails? By tying team responsibility to organizational performance, the systems of the organization begin to support the empowered efforts of the teams—indeed, to demand empowerment from the teams. Then the teams can begin to provide input into the individual goal setting and evaluation with an eye to the future when the teams will play a key role in individual performance management (including development and evaluation). Without this system expectation and support of the empowered teams, they may never become fully self-directed and empowered. Indeed, they may never even come close and, in so doing, may drag the empowerment effort to a halt.

One mobile telephone services company tried to cover all levels by having the bonus decision for each person based on performance at three levels—individual, team, and organization. If an individual reached his or her goals, that person received 50 percent of the allocated bonus. Another 25 percent was based on whether the individual's team met its goals, and the final 25 percent was based on whether the organization met its goals. The idea was to create a synergy between individual and team and between teams and organization. People were incentivized to work together on their teams and do their individual jobs well. The teams were "incentivized" to work together as an organization. This bonus system sent a very powerful message to people that paid big dividends in terms of team and organizational performance.

3. A valuable systems change is to reduce the number of departmental and staff meetings and to substitute team meetings in their place. If teams are to be held accountable for results, they will need off-line time to work together to identify problems and opportunities for improvement and to develop their skills for working together as an empowered team. Team leaders should be present at the meetings to provide direction and support as needed and to facilitate the development of the teams into self-directed units for performance and personnel development. Only by working together to achieve results and to grow as a unit in terms of team

competence and confidence will team members develop into a high performing self-directed team. And by restructuring the discussion from a departmental focus to a team focus, management enhances the movement toward empowerment, especially when people may be doubting the sincerity of the senior leadership for creating a culture of empowerment.

One organization that we followed for several years in the utility industry encountered some serious problems when it did not shift responsibility to the teams. The leaders shared information and changed the performance appraisal process, but the focus remained on the leader-team member relationship. The complaint from the people was that they were still not allowed to use their ideas. As one person put it, "The leaders say they are concerned about safety, but do they think we are not concerned about our own safety? Let us use our ideas and we'll work together to get the job done faster, better, and safely!"

What Problems Will the Teams Encounter during this Stage of Development, and How Can They Be

Assisted in Overcoming Those Problems?

1. One of the most debilitating problems teams can encounter in the valley of discouragement is a nagging fear of failure. When the inevitable snags are encountered during this second stage of the change-to-empowerment process, it is quite natural for team members to doubt themselves. But it is also typical for team members to place blame for their difficulties on their team leaders and on senior leadership. Team leaders can help the teams understand that this fear of failure is a natural occurrence along the journey to empowerment. All teams experience this concern, but by staying focused on the vision of an empowered team and working to improve their functioning as a team, they will overcome this feeling. Team leaders will need some coaching themselves on the best way to explain how and why this fear occurs. It occurs mainly because people are being asked to work in a different manner than in the past. Mistakes are to be expected, but in the past, mistakes have likely been unacceptable (at least in the minds of the team members). Hence, one of the most powerful changes leaders can make is to value mistakes as learning opportunities, not as omens of failure. Team leaders must not punish team members or teams when honest mistakes are made. Effort needs to be praised,

while people are helped to learn from their mistakes.

2. Teams will not yet be capable of performing at high levels of team efficiency. They have developed some of the skills of teamwork—group communication skills, information sharing, and some problem identification skills. But they still need to further develop the skills that lead to synergistic performance, such as reaching and supporting consensus decisions, sharing leadership, resolving conflicts among team members, and effective group listening. The lack of these skills will inhibit the teams in their ability to function. It is therefore important to provide additional team-building activities. Engage the teams in training opportunities that allow them to learn and practice team skills, using both experiential exercises and real work situations. Since some teams may be farther along than others in this growth process, it can also be useful to engage in some cross-team training activities. A side benefit may be that the teams have actual work issues that cut across the team boundaries, and these training activities will afford opportunities to address the issues in the context of a learning environment.

3. Because teams will tend to doubt their abilities at this point, it is crucial to their growth and development to help them again see their power for dealing with and solving complex problems.

Use simulations, as well as real world problems, to help team members and team leaders appreciate the power of empowered teams. Reinforcement with success is a powerful motivator for further development of the teams. Team leaders must continually seek opportunities to catch teams doing things well as a team and to then deliver positive feedback, which will be a powerful motivator for the team and its development.

CONCLUSION

At this juncture we have some ideas to help counter the negative forces of the valley of discouragement. Many organizations, and their leaders and team members, fall off the path to empowerment during this difficult stage of the change process, even though they do not have to fail. It is natural for people to begin having serious doubts about the veracity of empowerment. Team members doubt the leadership's sincerity, and the leadership doubts the people's ability to ever take responsibility for their actions, with team leaders caught somewhere in the middle. By using the actions covered in this chapter and the previous two, the power of sharing information, creating autonomy through boundaries, and replacing the hierarchy with self-directed teams can be used to address the problems brought on by Change and Discouragement. At the same time, these techniques help ensure that the empowerment process has a greatly improved chance of reaching the final stage of the journey. In the next section, we will turn our attention to this third phase of the empowerment journey, a phase marked by the realization of the dream of empowerment, albeit initially at a rather delicate level that leads to Adopting and Refining Empowerment.

STAGE THREE

ADOPTING AND REFINING EMPOWERMENT

As the process of changing to empowerment enters the third stage of Adopting and Refining Empowerment, the new values, practices, and attitudes start to be fully integrated. At this point it is often tempting for people to reduce their attention to the process and assume that all will be well from now on. The assumption is that empowerment can be put on autopilot, but to do so would seriously jeopardize all the efforts to this point. There still remain a number of questions in the minds of people, plus the need to refine and hone the empowerment skills that are not yet habits.

This honing of skills is much like the development of any new habit; take golf, for example. When you decide to adopt a new stance for hitting your approach shots, you go through a period of "letting go" or "unlearning" your old stance, which felt quite natural even if it was not too effective. As you begin to adopt the new stance, it is at first something you have to think about every time you stand over an approach shot. Eventually, with a great deal of practice at the driving range as well as on the golf course, you begin to take up the new stance without having to think about it. At this point you have adopted a new habit, but as long as you have to think about it every time you make an approach shot, you have still not arrived at the point of integration of the new stance.

Achieving empowerment skills is much like this analogy. For a long time you will have to exercise constant vigilance to continue to use the skills of empowerment, which you know and can use but only with attention to detail. In their book, *Everyone's a Coach,* Don Shula and Ken Blanchard describe this as "overlearning."[1] As a football coach, Shula always wanted his players so prepared to carry out their duties that they could go on autopilot. When they could do that, they could make something "big" happen because they did not have to consciously think about their basic responsibilities. To be empowered at a high level means acting empowered under pressure, without having to think about it.

In this section we will address some of the issues that relate to this integration process. As an overlay, Situational Leadership® II informs us that people at this stage of development will be cautious but capable performers (that is, moderate to high in competence but lacking in self-confidence—Development Level 3). They continue to need support, Leadership Style 3, to help build confidence and to solidify their empowerment skills. In the next three chapters, we will direct our attention one by one to each of the three keys to empowerment. Our first focus will be on using information sharing in more powerful ways now that empowerment is becoming a reality. Next, we will explore the refined use of boundaries that create autonomy, followed by a focus on how the self-directed teams finally reach their full potential. Our format will continue to be posing questions that leaders and team members have about empowerment at this stage of the process and then providing answers from our experience and the experience of our clients. Let us get started with information sharing in the stage of Adopting and Refining Empowerment.

CHAPTER 9

Key #1: Enhance Information Sharing to Drive Performance

For most people involved in the change-to-empowerment process, this third stage, Adopting and Refining Empowerment, comes as a breath of fresh air after the difficult stage of Change and Discouragement. And it is tempting for people to take their eyes off the vision of full empowerment, which is focused not only on involvement but also on responsibility and results. Empowered organizations involve far greater responsibility for everyone. They involve people voicing their opinions, disagreeing with each other, arguing for their positions, and feeling the pressure of performance responsibility. They also involve people feeling a sense of ownership, being listened to and understood, and making use of and further developing their talents. Sometimes people focus too heavily on these positives as they try to distance themselves from the previous stage of discouragement. The thought of the more uncomfortable aspects of being empowered is a little scary for some people, though they may have trouble voicing those concerns.

Even though many questions have been answered during the first two stages of the process, a number of questions remain on people's minds. Some of the questions are focused at the personal level, while others relate to a broader view outside the person, which is in itself a good sign for the empowerment process. What are some of those questions?

1. I've had some success with this empowerment thing, but will I be able to fully learn all that is needed in a culture of empowerment?
2. Is the effort to change really worth it; will the leadership really let us go all the way to empowerment? (And the leadership is likely wondering, Should we allow the process to go all the way; will more accountability be the end result?)
3. Are we really impacting company or site results in a positive manner?
4. Who is not yet on board with the change to empowerment and how do we get them more involved? Is there really consequence management for those who do not embrace the empowerment effort? How are they holding the rest of us back?
5. How can our team work together more effectively? What is inhibiting us from becoming a self-directed team?
6. How can we take on an even more significant role in the company's business? Can we get involved in strategic decisions?

The concerns model we described earlier in chapter 2 on Situational Leadership® II refers to these types of issues and concerns as impact, collaboration, and refinement concerns. What we witness at this stage of change is that information, personal, and implementation concerns are more under control, so people turn to impact and collaboration concerns and finally to refinement concerns. Let us begin to address some of the specific questions leaders and team members have about information sharing as we enter this final stage of the journey to empowerment.

How Can Information Continue to Drive the Process As Empowerment Is Reaching Fruition?

1. At this point in the process, the teams are beginning to really use the information that has been shared with them. Because of that experience, they will also be in a position to become more involved in determining what information is really needed by the teams to enhance their performance. It is time to ask the teams how they are using the information they currently have about site and company performance. Ask if they need additional information on particular issues, less information on others, or information in a different format or a different time frame. What other kind of information do they want? These questions will help senior leadership and the teams ensure that they are placing value and importance on the same information and using the same measures

to track success. If there are inconsistencies between the information being used by the teams and by senior leadership, the result will be wasted efforts. It is critical for the teams to be clear on what information is most closely related to the goals of the company, but at this stage, it is also important for senior leadership to really listen to what the teams feel is important to measure relative to those goals.

One company in the packaging business eventually gave complete control to a number of teams throughout the company. Each team was set up as a little company within the larger company. The teams controlled the information-sharing process, asking for what they needed and generating a great deal of their own information. Once a quarter, the teams all came together to share their results for the quarter and to relate them to the overall company performance. The combined reports of the teams were rolled up into a company profit and loss statement for the quarter, along with other key measures of performance such as waste, machine downtime, packages shipped, turnover, and cost per unit of production. Through an open dialogue at these meetings, everyone learned what key measures were being used to assess company performance and what new ones might be needed to enhance accuracy.

2. The issue of trust between leadership and teams will continually need to be addressed. As the teams ask for more and more sensitive information, the leadership may be tempted to limit some forms or types of information. It is critical to the long-term success of the empowerment effort to trust the teams with whatever information they feel they need. If leaders feel the information is particularly sensitive or could be damaging in the hands of competition, they need to say that and then trust the teams to guard the information just as much as senior leadership would. It is certainly in the teams' best interest to do so. After coming this far in the empowerment journey, do not let a perceived lack of trust over information derail the effort.

3. Find out from the teams why they need additional information or need information more quickly. The point here is not to question the decisions of the team but rather to help the teams inform senior leadership about their thinking and their use of information. The teams are focusing primarily on operational matters and most likely want the new or more timely information to help them make more responsible decisions relative to business outcomes. By allowing them to explain their thinking, the teams will feel even more like partners in running the business. Just because senior leadership has not been using a certain type of information in its assessments of the

business does not mean that it should not be used in the future. The key factor here is to let the teams begin to control the information they need, while ensuring that both the teams and the leadership are on the same information "page."

4. The flip side of needing additional information must also be validated. At this stage, the teams have more experience with using information and knowing what information they need to achieve their goals. What they may decide is that some of the information they have been receiving is just not needed. By identifying what information is not needed, the teams can help to streamline the information-sharing process. These needs may change as problems are solved, goals are achieved, and issues are addressed by the teams.

One of our clients had recently won the coveted Deming quality award. The process of applying for the award had led the people to collect great volumes of data. In fact, they had become so used to collecting data they were gathering it on almost everything they did. For example, they measured the response time of the receptionists for over a year and found a very steady pattern. Response time dropped off between 11:30a.m. and 12:30p.m. and between 1:00p.m. and 2:00p.m. They found that response time was slower when one of the two receptionists went on a lunch break and was faster when both were present. Nobody had bothered to ask if that slowing of response time actually created a problem. When the receptionists found it did not create a problem, they stopped collecting this useless data. If, on the other hand, the slower response time had created a problem, they could have identified a measure of the problem and begun to address it.

5. Certainly, by this point in the process, some changes should already have been made in the information technology system. Perhaps the system produces more of the kind of information the teams need and in a more timely fashion, but what now? Can we make the information available on a real-time basis on demand by the teams? Can the teams easily access the information they need? Can changes be made easily in the system to accommodate the desires of the teams without undue delay? In other words, make the information technology a flexible tool for giving the teams the information they need to effectively make decisions and solve problems that translate into a higher level of performance for the site and company.

A retail clothing company set a goal for building an information technology system that would allow a person anywhere in the organization to have immediate access to any information needed. The leaders also wanted to make the information available in as close to real time as possible. Naturally, this meant having a system that allowed daily updates and that allowed anyone from the top to the bottom of the organization to access the same information. A great deal of effort was put into achieving this goal, and it has not been easy. Still, significant progress has been made and the commitment to reaching this state of information fluidity has not been sacrificed. The effort has made people throughout the organization more committed to using, to the best of their capabilities, the information they can access.

Is Information Sharing As Vital Now As It Was at the Beginning of the Journey to Empowerment?

1. Information sharing is every bit as important now as it was at the beginning of the journey—but for different reasons. At the beginning, information sharing jump-started the process of building responsibility and trust. Prior to the empowerment efforts, people did not have access to the information needed to make responsible business decisions; hence they did not make those decisions.

Furthermore, by being kept in the dark, people felt that leaders did not trust them, and they returned the favor with distrust. Information sharing began to change those dynamics. Now information sharing is vital to continuing to build responsibility and to enhance the trust relationship.

2. Information sharing is a vital element for the fully empowered organization. Information sharing is the key tool to drive continuous improvement. In an empowered company, people want the ongoing challenge of getting better and better at their work. They recognize that continuous improvement is the means for keeping the company healthy and competitive. But they also recognize that it is the means for success, satisfaction, and fulfillment in their jobs and careers. Information sharing is, quite simply, the lifeblood of an empowered organization. Without it, a company can never become or stay fully empowered.

One company in the metal finishing business tackled this issue in an interesting way. Because the company was unionized, the company leadership did not feel comfortable sharing *all* information initially, especially since the commencement of the empowerment process coincided with contract negotiations with the union. Our advice was to start slow by sharing a little of the less-threatening information. When this was followed by a positive response from the rank and file, as well as from the union leadership, the leadership was encouraged to share more information. Over time, the leadership has continued to increase the sharing of information, and the result has been a better partnership among the leaders, team members, and union. Empowerment is slowly taking place in this company, driven in large part by better and better information sharing.

3. Information sharing is the mechanism by which people can be held accountable for achieving goals and for achieving them at higher standards of performance. Sharing information is also the mechanism by which people and teams can *hold themselves accountable* for progress toward their goals. Furthermore, shared information (and free access to information) is the key mechanism by which people and teams can track progress toward desired outcomes and then *manage themselves* toward those outcomes. With information, people and teams can change plans, know when to work harder or smarter, be aware of impending problems, and know when to celebrate progress toward goals. They can also begin to be true partners with senior leadership by focusing on important issues such as how to better serve both internal and external customers. Customers today expect a great deal from their service providers,

and without customers who feel a high level of service, any unit or organization will soon suffer. Indeed, what teams need to develop, and can develop at this stage, is *Raving Fan* customers—people who are so pleased with the way they are treated that they brag about their service providers. If a team takes on the goal of Raving Fan service, it can benefit by using the three steps described below and outlined by Ken Blanchard and Sheldon Bowles in their book on the topic.[2]

When the team members focus on the first step—Decide What You Want—they determine how they want to operate. For example, will they use recovery as a customer service strategy for dealing with customer disappointments, or are they willing to change rules that prevent great service and allow team members the autonomy to create Raving Fan customers? When the attention turns to the second step—Discover What the Customer Wants—they must be willing to measure service with the same passion that is used to measure profit and loss. And they must be willing to accept what they hear from customers. A useful tool in this process is the Raving Fans Gap Finder, which asks customers to rate the team on a variety of measures, compare the team on these measures to other similar teams, and declare the importance of these measures.[3] The third step—Deliver Plus One—allows the team to become involved directly in implementing a plan to create Raving Fan cus-

244

tomers. The power of this approach is that people are empowered to address important business issues. In the past, all of these actions would have been considered the responsibility of the management hierarchy, but they are now the challenge for teams and individuals in an empowered organization.

CREATING RAVING FANS

1. Decide What You Want
The team must decide what its commitment to service will look like.

2. Discover What the Customer Wants
The team must continually listen to the customer to learn what is important and how its service is rated.

3. Deliver Plus One
The team must close the service gaps and develop a plan for improving service that exceeds customer expectations by one percent over and over again.

Ken Blanchard and Sheldon Bowles, *Raving Fans: A Revolutionary Approach to Customer Service* (New York: William Morrow and Company, 1993), 22, 51, 101.

What Must Be Done to Deal with the Ever Changing Face of the workforce?

1. One of the issues that comes up in any change effort is what to do about new people who join the organization after the process is underway. The issues are, of course, different if we are talking about a person coming from outside the company versus someone coming from another location within the company. Someone from outside the organization must be indoctrinated into the entire empowerment process—what it means in this company, the history of the change process, the new expectations in the culture of empowerment, the information-sharing requirements, the current boundaries of operation, and the development stage of the teams. Someone coming from another location will know the general characteristics in the company, but he or she will need to know the specifics of the new location regarding information sharing, boundaries, and team effort. The team charter, which we described in chapter 5, can be a valuable mechanism for sharing this information with new team members, regardless of whether they are coming from inside or outside the company.

A good example of this process on the company level is the Disney corporation. Every new employee,

246

including the CEO, must go through the "traditions" program. Here people learn the organization's values and history. They learn what the expectations are for everyone, and they develop an appreciation for the pride that all members share. In another company, Armstrong Industries, an oversized storybook was created covering key policies, values, and expectations. Visitors to the company, vendors, and new employees are encouraged to look at the book. The message that is implied is If you want to do business with us or work here, you might want to (need to) read our storybook first. This sends a powerful and clear message that is helpful to new members of the organization.

2. Since information sharing was the key for kick-starting the process for the organization and beginning to build responsibility and trust for the culture of empowerment, it is a logical first step for a new person, as well. Teach the new person the values and expectations regarding information in this culture. Just as at the beginning of the process, this explanation will facilitate the integration of the new person into the culture of empowerment in the company. Explain to the new person what kinds of information are shared, how they are shared, how frequently they are shared, and

what his or her personal responsibility is regarding this information. Also explain the expectations about sharing information that is in one's possession.

3.   Continue sharing information as a means of keeping everyone knowledgeable about what is happening throughout the organization. Just as the environment surrounding the company will change, so will the people in the company. Here we are talking about the people who have been involved since the beginning of the change-to-empowerment process. We sometimes forget that people are changed along this journey to empowerment. At the beginning they were accustomed to working in a hierarchical culture. Now they are becoming comfortable with working in a culture of empowerment. They understand that their roles and the expectations of them are quite different, and they expect different behaviors from the organization's senior leadership and their team leaders. With a value and practice of continuously sharing information with team members and expecting them to share with team leaders and senior leadership, people in the organization will continue to mature into a highly skilled culture of empowerment that achieves outstanding results and stays ahead of the competition.

How Do You Deal with the Problem of Information Getting Stuck Somewhere in the Organization?

1. In a culture of empowerment, it is important to ensure that everyone from senior leadership through middle management to team members knows that information sharing is a strong value. Therefore, people who do a good job of sharing information should be acknowledged for conforming to the values of empowerment. Those who fail to share information must be reminded in clear terms that such hoarding of information is not acceptable in the new culture. Indeed, senior leadership must be sure that no one is hoarding or can hoard information and not pass it along to others in the company. One way to do this is for senior leadership to continually ask team members if they have all the information they feel they need to improve performance, while also thinking about what additional information senior leadership feels would be helpful to the team members. These strategies will help keep the communication channels open throughout the organization. And when people do not have the information they need, ask them if they know where it is located, and if not, then find out where it is and make it available to the teams.

2. A very powerful strategy that will impact information sharing, as well as many of the other desired behaviors of an empowered culture, is to reward those team members and leaders who exemplify the behaviors of the new culture. Such rewards do not need to be financial in nature. Rather, a public recognition with clarity about what is being praised will help to solidify the kind of information sharing that will keep the organization moving toward full empowerment status. On the other hand, when people do not exhibit the desired information-sharing behaviors, they must be reminded in clear terms that not sharing or not using information is unacceptable in the new culture of empowerment. By clearly differentiating the treatment of people who promote empowerment from those who do not, the empowerment process can continue to move toward full integration into the practices, behaviors, and attitudes of everyone in the organization.

3. Continue to encourage people to share information about mistakes that are made so that everyone can learn from the mistakes and so that an effective solution can be found and implemented. Remember, in an empowered culture we want people to share information that tells both good and bad stories. When information is shared that says, "We have a problem," then everyone can get involved in finding creative solutions. Additionally, information that tells a bad story can help

identify problems at an early stage when less damage has been done and when easier solutions will fix the problem. The result is better performance of the company and location that is dealing with problems in an empowered way.

One of the companies with which we have worked developed an interesting way to reward people who identified a system or policy problem and acted in a way to work around the problem to serve a customer. Many companies give "Eagle Awards" when people soar above the call of duty. This company used the opposite concept of "ducking" problems and hiding behind a policy as an excuse for not serving a customer. They created a "Duck Award" to be given to a person who used good judgment by ignoring a "dumb policy or rule." Such action both served the customer at the moment and also identified a policy or system problem to be fixed by the organization. These awards recognized team members as partners who could identify company boundaries that inhibited them from acting empowered. They also reinforced the empowerment efforts of both team members and leaders.

4. Information sharing can also become derailed, depending on how the information is gathered and used. The result can be that information gets stuck coming up the organization from team

members. The problem typically starts with a senior leadership request for data and reports from the front line that creates a hardship on the team members in the collection process. In addition, the front line may not see the value of the information that it is being asked to collect. The channels of communication need to be kept open so that such problems are identified early and do not become inhibitors of information sharing.

A convenience store chain encountered this problem when it created serious inhibitors to empowerment. Senior leadership wanted to track weekly inventory of various sizes of cups against reported sales. The method developed by headquarters staff was to have the front line hand count the "tubes" daily and complete a form that was collected by supervisors daily. This task required twenty minutes of extra work for the frontline people, and the front line believed that the leadership was doing it only to track shrinkage (employee theft). The people "got even" of course by creating overtime to count cups, acting on their perceived lack of trust from senior leadership. One of the senior vice presidents from operations finally took an incredible action to support his frontline team. He notified the headquarters staff that they would communicate with his store managers only through him and that no requests or policies were to be made until he approved them.

Finance, accounting, legal, marketing, purchasing, and warehouse all had protested. But they had created the problem by inventing a solution that made their job easier and the job of the front line harder. Better communication was needed to rebuild the trust that had been shaken.

CONCLUSION

Now that we have entered the final stage of creating a culture of empowerment by using information sharing, we must again be reminded that the other two keys play equally important roles in finalizing all the effort in the process. It takes refined use of declaring the boundaries for autonomy and replacing the hierarchy with self-directed teams to complete the journey. Thus, in the next chapter we will turn our attention to how boundaries can enhance the creation of autonomy in this stage of Adopting and Refining Empowerment.

CHAPTER 10

Key #2: Incorporate Boundaries into Everyone's Value System

All along the journey to empowerment we have had to be aware of utilizing the three keys as a package to promote change. This final stage is no different from the first two, except that now more of the guidance from boundaries comes from within the people. People are now asking for the information they need and making good use of that information. The boundaries that guide behavior in the empowered culture are much wider than at the beginning of the journey. The challenge is to take the last step of incorporating the boundaries fully into the value systems of the people in the organization. Managers have come a long way toward becoming team leaders, just as the people have progressed far toward being team members. That is not to suggest, however, that boundaries are no longer needed to guide autonomous actions. Rather, it is to suggest that the locus of the boundaries needs to be moved as much as possible into the hands and minds of the team members. Let us turn to responding to the questions that are typically on the minds of people at this stage of the journey to empowerment.

How Do We Use Boundaries Now That We Are Becoming Fully Empowered?

1. The vision of what the organization will look like as an empowered company needs to be refined to reflect progress to date. At the beginning of the process, employees (now team members) were asked to take on the more simple decisions that affected their work (e.g., maintaining safety and housekeeping, measuring customer service and quality, and selecting work methods). As the journey progressed, the team members began to take on more complex decisions (e.g., determining training needs, routine equipment repair, cross-training needs, and production scheduling). The vision of the decision making of the company must be refined to reflect the scope and depth of the types of decisions that people are now making. The vision must also be reshaped to provide new focus for the future direction of the empowerment efforts. In the domain of decision making, the teams must be challenged to take on an even more expanded scope and complexity of decisions. For example, they may need to decide when and how to engage in cross-function teaming, who to hire for new positions, how to handle individual performance problems, and how to prepare bud-

gets. This final stage of the empowerment process must integrate most of the old hierarchical decision-making practices into the self-directed teams' practices.

A company in the food manufacturing and distribution business went so far as to eliminate traditional functions such as personnel, finance, engineering, maintenance, and training. All of these activities, which are handled in "silos" in hierarchical organizations, were now the domain of the teams. The self-directed teams had replaced the old hierarchical decision-making practices. They made budgeting decisions, maintained their own equipment, solved production problems, and conducted all the training (or arranged for it) for their own team members.

2. Many, if not all, of the old hierarchical boundaries must be replaced with vision and values that reside within the people. As we have discussed earlier, hierarchical boundaries are typically used to define *what cannot be done,* as well as what procedures must be followed related to taking certain actions. The boundaries in a culture of empowerment define for people the *areas within which they have freedom to operate* and are expected to take autonomous action to achieve results. In this final stage of the empowerment journey, the boundaries are widened to allow for

greater autonomy and responsibility of the teams and their members. Team leaders have to make very clear the vision for action and responsibility and the values that guide that action. They must also continue to work with the teams to incorporate these boundaries into the beliefs and attitudes of everyone involved. Team leaders have to continue to build empowered teams and then to trust and expect that what they have built will work.

A great visual analogy that we use in our work with companies is to have people think of the sidelines of a football field and then ask them, "Who has the widest playing field (boundaries) in the company?" In a hierarchy it is clearly the CEO, and each level of management down the hierarchy has a smaller playing field. By the time you get to the front line people, the playing field can be very narrow, indeed. In the empowerment process, these boundaries have been gradually widened as people have learned to act with responsibility and use their skills to get the work done. By this final stage, the boundaries may still not be as wide as those for the CEO, but they are much, much wider than they were when the process began. The boundaries provide guidelines for the autonomy of all members of the organization, and they also build responsibility into the values of every person in the company.

The leaders in a financial services company learned during the second stage of the change-to-empowerment process that their confusion and uncertainty was often the perfect opportunity to allow more input and responsibility from the teams. By the time they reached the third stage of the process, the managers (now team leaders) were quite comfortable with trusting the teams to make good decisions and to create innovative solutions to problems. The reduction in pressure perceived by the team leaders was a most welcome outcome, as were the ideas that led to reduced costs and better service for customers. Many of the team leaders reported the pleasure of being able to spend more time with their families.

3. In focusing on the refinement of vision and values, it is important to include team members as full partners in the process. At the beginning of the journey, they needed clear boundaries set for them, but now they can help assess and reestablish boundaries to guide their efforts and decision making. Team leaders and team members should work together to look for ways to enhance the empowerment process. By sharing ideas about the vision and values, the organization will benefit from both a wider network for ideas and a stronger sense of commitment to ideas that are adopted. As is so often the case,

the ideas of team members can surpass those of management when it comes to operational decisions that impact bottom-line results, quality, and customer satisfaction.

One retail company creates this sense of partnership in its handbook, which is given to all team members. It says, "You were hired for your good judgment. We expect and assume you will use it in dealing with our customers within the philosophy of our company." It then declares, "There are no other rules." Team members are taught to respond to customer problems with an attitude and action that says, "No problem. We can and will get the problem fixed." Obviously, such statements provide very broad guidelines for partnership action. They represent just how wide boundaries can grow in the final stage of the journey.

4. While boundaries are set to create guidelines within which freedom can occur, we must remember that they are also set to establish responsibilities for action and outcomes. At this stage of the change-to-empowerment process, team members should be more comfortable with taking more responsibility. They should be less fearful of making mistakes but more keenly aware of the need to continue to learn from mistakes. Without such learning, the organization and its people will suf-

fer in the competitive business world that sur-rounds them. Hence, it is critical at this stage to continue to reinforce both the freedom and the responsibility that go with empowerment.

5. When conflicts arise on the teams, it is important not to squash the conflicts to protect team member egos. Indeed, conflict of ideas must be nurtured so that the diversity of talents can help the teams deal with the complex problems they face. The real key is to let values be the determi-nants of action and the guidelines that clarify decision making. At this stage, when values should be clear to everyone, decision making will be easier if it is guided by these values.

What Should Be the Focus of Goals That Are Set in the Emerging Culture of Empowerment?

1. By this stage of the change-to-empowerment process, team goals should have almost replaced individual goals, as far as the company is con-cerned. From an organizational perspective, the self-directed teams are the vehicle for achieving the company's goals and objectives. Hence, cor-porate goals and objectives that are consistent with the strategy must be translated into goals for the teams in a collaborative process among senior leadership, team leaders, and team mem-bers. The self-directed teams accept the respon-

sibility for these goals, and then they can establish individual goals for team members in another collaborative process that ensures each team member knows what must be done to assist the team in meeting its goals.

2. Since the self-directed teams take on the responsibility for achievement of goals that drive business results, they must also take on the task of monitoring progress toward those goals and making the necessary adjustments. This, of course, means that the teams will use information to track performance and to assess the impact of actions they take. They will also need to ask for any additional information they feel is necessary for goal accomplishment. Finally, this responsibility means that the teams will have to monitor goal progress by each member of the team. It will be the team's responsibility to ensure that individual team members are staying on track so that the team as a whole stays on track for high performance.

A bank found this approach to responsibility and accountability very troublesome at first. The history of a culture that gave feedback only when people made mistakes created a discomfort with team members' giving each other feedback. What helped them eventually get over this hurdle was a focus on clear goals and measures that allowed much greater

self-monitoring. The team members could then primarily focus on giving positive feedback to their
colleagues, while encouraging team members to ask
for help when they saw they were having trouble
reaching their individual goals. Gradually, the teams
developed the ability to control and monitor themselves, primarily because they shifted the culture to
one of positive feedback first and then problem
solving, rather than blaming when things were not
going well.

3. In the new culture of empowerment, the teams
    must be allowed to establish any goals they feel
    will help them contribute to the site's or compa-
    ny's achievement of its strategic goals. Strategic
    goals must still be set in clear terms by the senior
    leadership team. The leadership will, however,
    want to make full use of any input that the teams
    can provide. With the teams' commitment to and
    understanding of the strategic goals of the site
    or company, the teams can act responsibly in
    setting their goals. They must be trusted as em-
    powered teams to set goals that are achievable
    and that move the organization toward its
    strategic goals.
4. During the entire process of moving toward em-
    powerment, the focus has been on achieving
    continuous improvement. At this stage, people
    should be much more comfortable with this aspect

of never-ending performance improvement expectations. Indeed, the teams should be at a point where they can identify many areas for improvement that relate to operational matters and ultimately to strategic goal accomplishment. The teams must be encouraged—indeed, expected—to set continuous improvement goals for every process in which they are involved. Typically, the pride they have developed in achieving more and more complex goals will provide the energy to continue to tackle improvement goals, but encouragement and praise from team leaders and senior leadership can also enhance the efforts of the teams.

5. At this stage of the process, it is critical for teams to remember that goals without agreement are mandates and therefore the antithesis of empowerment. The efforts to move toward collaborative goal setting that have marked the first two stages of the change-to-empowerment process must not be neglected at this stage. Team members now expect to be involved in the process of evaluating information, identifying problems or opportunities, and then setting goals. They are well versed in setting operational goals by this point and are ready to become involved in assessments of information and goal setting related to company strategic directions. Collaborative goal setting is one of the most critical elements of building and reinforcing the partnership among

senior leadership, team leaders, and team members that typifies empowerment.

How Should the Performance Management Process Look at This Point in the Process?

1. At the beginning of the change-to-empowerment process, the organization most likely had a once-a-year appraisal process that relied heavily on a form and on data that was less than complete. *As the empowerment journey has unfolded, the performance appraisal process has given way to a performance management process that is ongoing throughout the year.* Such a process complements the empowerment challenge since it relies heavily on collaborative goals as a starting point, followed by ongoing coaching that is guided by information related to goal progress, followed by a review step that is a true partnership centered on evaluation and learning for the future. At this final stage of the journey, the teams must begin to take over the performance management process. Senior leadership should work with the teams, focusing on team goal setting, coaching, and reviewing in this process. In turn, the teams must manage their internal performance management process. By that we mean that the teams should set individual goals for team members at the beginning of a performance cycle. Then during

the cycle, the teams must share information and monitor the performance of each of their members, with the members engaging in a great deal of self-monitoring as well. At the end of the cycle, the teams must review their performance as a team both among themselves and with senior leadership, and they must review the contributions of each member of the team with an eye toward improvement in the future. The key point here is that the teams run their own internal performance management process, while the senior leadership interacts with the teams via a team-based performance management process that encircles the internal team process. Such interlocking activities build ongoing collaboration and responsibility at the individual level, the team level, and the organizational level, and they make for an alignment of effort that drives high levels of organizational performance.

2. An integral part of the performance management process is the decision package that focuses on staffing concerns. In an empowered culture, the self-directed teams should begin to make many of the decisions that are made by the human resources function of a hierarchical organization. These include hiring, disciplining, and firing decisions that relate to the team members, as well as decisions regarding scheduling overtime and administering skill-based pay programs.

In a manufacturing company in the Southeast, the traditional human resources (HR) function was retained to handle paperwork, record-keeping, and payroll, but the teams made hiring and firing decisions with the support of HR. Candidates for jobs were initially screened by HR using criteria provided by the teams. Then candidates were interviewed by team members who made the final decision and made offers to the candidates. New team members were briefed on some of the general company matters by HR, but the bulk of their orientation and training was handled by the teams themselves. The teams also handled disciplining of their team members and were authorized to fire members who did not perform, under the guidance of HR to protect them from legal repercussions.

3. Allow and expect the teams to hold themselves accountable for progress toward goal accomplishment. It should also be the responsibility of the teams to keep senior leadership informed of their progress and of any signs of being off track for successful goal achievement. *Early in each performance cycle, the teams and their team leaders must agree with senior leadership on the set of measures that will be used to track performance.* Clarity on these measures defines in operational terms what is important and also defines the boundaries of team effort. The teams can act

autonomously within the vision and values of the organization to achieve the goals, as tracked by the agreed-upon measures. Other measures that are not tracked define what is not important, unless experience during the process suggests a redefining of key performance measures. The key point here is to get everyone on the same measurement "page" since this agreement will create a coordinated effort that is both efficient and effective in achieving results. In today's competitive world, focusing people's energy to maximize their use of time becomes a critical variable that may determine a company's success or failure. Hence, the effort to align measures that allow the teams to be self-monitoring and accountable and that allow them to hold their members accountable becomes vital in a world of empowerment.

4. Our experience suggests that any performance management system where a team member learns new information about his or her performance at the time of the review is a system that is not working. A critical measure for assessing whether a company's performance management system is working for empowerment is whether there are any "surprises" at the end of the performance cycle. An effective system should involve continual updating and monitoring from both the team member and the team leader. New information during the cycle may suggest that goals or coaching strategy be adjusted. By making these

adjustments in a collaborative partnership between the team member and the team leader, the performance management system will generate a sense of validation that comes from a consistency of collaborative effort and information sharing over time.

Can the Boundaries for New Business Operating Procedures Be Widened?

1. As we enter the final stage of the journey to empowerment, teams can become true partners with management by being encouraged to help create new business opportunities. Most of their effort has been, and will remain, focused on the operational issues surrounding accomplishment of the strategic goals set by senior leadership. Empowerment primarily focuses on helping the organization serve its customers more effectively, cut costs, maintain efficiency, and act flexibly in reacting to external demands. But in an empowered organization, the line between some of these issues, from both operational and strategic points of view, can and should become blurred. For example, serving customers more effectively can be narrowly defined as producing the requested product in a timely, low cost, and high quality fashion. It could be more broadly defined as researching product variations or related products that customers want and then providing those

new products in a timely, low cost, and high quality fashion. Companies that are fully empowered ask for new product ideas and new strategic direction ideas from everyone in the organization, just as much as they ask for operational improvements from everyone.

A medium-sized food processing and sales company listened to a secretary about an idea she had for developing a new market for the company's products. Prior to her suggestion, the company had sold only to wholesalers, who in turn sold to grocery stores. The secretary suggested starting a catalogue business to provide an additional direct avenue to customers. She was encouraged to pursue the idea, and after one year, the catalogue business she was running had grown to over a million dollars with the promise of growing far beyond that size.

2. Encourage the self-directed teams to continually look for ways to refine operational practices to enhance profitability. Since the teams are working with the production and service delivery mechanisms on a daily basis, they are in the best position to identify problems with, and make improvements to, the operations of the business. Using the information at their disposal, they can assess waste, machine downtime, time for service delivery, and so forth. Then, using their knowledge,

experience, and motivation, they will be able to determine means for improving a variety of operational measures. Indeed, such improvements should be a stated value of the organization so there is no misunderstanding of the importance of this focus. Likewise, improvements should be a part of the performance management process and should be tied to compensation decisions. Let us add one caution at this point. It is critical to make it easy for teams to develop and implement their ideas. Make sure that you do not encumber the process with lots of bureaucratic red tape and procedures. A streamlined process for new ideas—with results as the key measure of success—is what companies should be trying to create.

One manufacturing company in the paper products industry used teams to focus explicitly on operational improvements. By providing information on performance and training on how to operate as effective teams, they were able to reduce waste by 30 percent and increase throughput by 20 percent, while reducing turnover of personnel to almost nothing. To achieve these outstanding results, the teams engaged in budget decisions, they tackled production problems, they felt they owned the business, and they worked as cohesive units in a most responsible fashion.

3. The self-directed teams must now fully realize the concept of being business partners with management. Frontline team members, team leaders, and senior leadership must begin to act like true equals in terms of accepting responsibility for the success of the organization. Positive and negative feedback on performance can flow up, down, and sideways in the organization. Frontline people can provide ideas to senior leadership and expect action, just as senior leadership can expect response from frontline team members. Information sharing flows in all directions, originating from whatever source is most appropriate and responded to by whatever source is appropriate. For example, frontline people are closer to the action of production or service delivery. Hence, they may observe events or collect data that are unavailable to senior leadership. As partners, it is their job to share that information with team leaders, members of other teams, and senior leadership. It is also their responsibility to act on information as appropriate in terms of making decisions to fix or improve conditions and then informing others of what they have done. Business partners work together for the good of the empowered organization, and partner actions must be encouraged and expected by all parties at this stage of the journey.

4. At this stage of the change-to-empowerment process, the self-directed teams should feel fully empowered to take bold action to improve the business. This action, of course, includes many operational and strategic initiatives that are within their control. It can also begin to include the creation of "stretch" goals for senior leadership. Perhaps the teams will see and push for new strategic initiatives that senior management has not considered. Or perhaps they will push for investments that their analysis shows will enhance production, quality, or cost measures. The key point is not to be surprised if teams become the initiators and pushers for bold action as they become fully empowered. A convenient framework for understanding the journey that has been made by this stage is the one provided by Trevor Keighley and his colleagues in Australia and described in chapter 8.[1] The framework focuses on the types of decisions the teams make and how they make them. In this final stage of the change effort, the teams decide and take action within clear boundaries without consulting leaders and management beforehand. The teams have the authority and responsibility to make important business decisions and are held accountable for the outcomes of those decisions.

CONCLUSION

With this discussion of the refined use of boundaries to create autonomy added to the refined use of information sharing from the previous chapter, we are now ready to focus on the use of the third key (replacing the hierarchy with self-directed teams). As we have mentioned several times before, completing the journey to empowerment takes all three keys working in harmony. In the next chapter, we will explore how the empowered teams can be fully adopted and refined, as well as how this effort will help us take the last steps to a new culture of empowerment.

CHAPTER 11

Key #3: Let Teams Replace the Hierarchy

As we are now in this final stage of the journey to empowerment, we want to make full use of the power of replacing the hierarchy with self-directed teams to achieve full empowerment. During the first two stages of the change process, the teams have gone through a period of Orientation where they were trying to determine what it would mean to be part of an empowered team. They have also gone through a period of Dissatisfaction where team members wondered if they would not be better off working as individuals in this new empowerment culture. Entering this final stage of changing to empowerment, the teams are coming to Integration, where they have resolved the issues that have held them back from becoming an empowered team. They are gelling as a team capable of extremely high levels of performance. Indeed, they are reaching the stage of Production, where they can take on many of the roles that management performs in a traditional hierarchy. The questions that remain revolve around these final steps to self-directed status and concern refining and reinforcing what the teams are capable of doing. Let us explore some of the questions that are typical of this stage of the process and that relate to the teams.

How Do the Teams Truly Replace Many of the Old Functions of the Management Hierarchy?

1. The teams now possess information that prior to the empowerment effort was almost exclusively in the hands of management. They also have a clear vision and a set of operational values. The teams are thus positioned to play a vital role in the organization. By combining information with clear boundaries and team skills, the teams can draw on their collective knowledge, experience, and motivation to achieve impressive results. More specifically, they can now make the complex decisions of broad scope that a team leader has previously made. For example, they can handle new team member interviewing and hiring, conduct team member performance evaluations, handle individual performance problems, prepare and monitor budgets, and arrange for equipment purchases. Indeed, with information and clear boundaries, the self-directed teams can identify problem areas or potential problem areas and initiate plans for resolving the problems. All they need now, according to Situational Leader-

ship® II, is continued encouragement to help them cross into the stage where they have team competence and feel confident in each other to fully use their talents.

A company in the pollution control design field initially found it difficult to make this shift in responsibility. The team members could vividly recall the previous stage of Dissatisfaction and did not like the idea of having to deal with performance problems of team members. Their solution was to focus on clear expectations and work hard to avoid performance problems. What they found was that performance problems occurred less frequently than in the past, and they were easier to resolve because they were spotted earlier and because the expectations were very clear from the beginning.

2. Teams should begin to hold themselves accountable for understanding company strategic goals, tracking the same information that senior leadership tracks relative to these strategic goals, and setting team goals that link to the accomplishment of strategic goals. Teams should even begin interpreting information and offering suggestions to leadership. In support of this responsibility, senior leadership should make it clear that the teams are expected to take on

this more analytical and strategic activity. In addition, it is time for the teams to embrace the responsibility for innovation and new ideas that reduce cost, increase quality, increase productivity, improve customer service, or enhance flexibility. In other words, the self-directed teams should now become responsible "leaders" of key business outcomes.

In one telecommunications company, teams were created and charged with assessing production methods and then making and implementing suggestions for improvement. The teams started slowly with very few suggestions, but the suggestions did have an impact. Within two years, the number of suggestions had grown to more than five per employee per year, which far exceeded the national average for number of suggestions. Furthermore, the number of ideas implemented increased very quickly to exceed 60 percent, more than six times the national average. And the suggestions that were implemented saved hundreds of thousands of dollars. Perhaps more important was the change in attitude of the workforce. One team member was quoted as saying, "It doesn't matter what name is on the plaque outside, this company belongs to me and my team as much as it belongs to anyone."

How Do Teams Maintain Themselves as High-Involvement, Empowered Teams?

1. One of the most important challenges facing a self-directed team that has reached the level of an empowered team is staying at that level, especially as new members join the team, perhaps because someone else has departed. The team must recognize that a new member puts the team back into the orientation issues it faced at the beginning of the team development process. Especially with regard to a new person, time must be spent providing that person with the direction and clarity of how this team operates and how this person must adapt to the team. But the team must also reorient itself on how to work with this new member instead of the departed member. If the two people are quite different in style and skills, the team will have more trouble with this integration process, but nevertheless, it must occur if the team is to stay empowered. In chapter 5, where the focus was on teams at the first stage of the change process, we made reference to the PERFORM model for describing and assessing a team's high performing status. Each letter in the acronym identifies a characteristic of a high performing empowered team:

P=Purpose and Values
E=Empowerment

R=Relationships and Communication
F=Flexibility
O=Optimal performance
R=Recognition and Appreciation
M=Morale

In this final stage of the change process, where the focus is on adopting and refining empowerment, the teams will be able to see the PERFORM elements affect the practices of individuals, teams, management, and the organization.

2. Another more subtle aspect of keeping self-directed teams functioning effectively is the recognition of how the same individual team members may change. Over time, people may adopt different attitudes and opinions through personal growth and development, and the team will have to continue to work at staying highly empowered. Often, this work depends on team members staying flexible as they change, keeping communications about attitude and personal issues relatively open on the team, and keeping the vision of an empowered team in plain view for all team members to see. Maintaining a well-oiled team machine is like keeping up any piece of equipment; it takes time, focus, and effort. Otherwise, the team will gradually lose its ability to stay self-directed.

One highly empowered company in software engineering followed a practice of having periodic team retreats to maintain the teams at a high level of proficiency. The retreats gave the teams time off from their hectic work schedules to keep up with changes in each person that might affect the team. The retreats also allowed the team to more fully integrate new members and to refocus everyone's efforts on the challenges facing the company and the teams. Renewed energy and focus always followed the retreats and helped the teams maintain an edge in their capabilities to perform and improve.

3. Teams must be encouraged to extend their range of influence. No doubt some teams will move more quickly toward empowerment than others. By reaching out to other teams, they can positively influence the other teams to continue their journey to empowerment. By spreading word of their success, self-directed teams can demonstrate to the company how an empowered team can have positive results and also be an exciting place to be involved. Indeed, one of the most exciting observations concerning empowered teams is problem solving and decision making that includes multiple teams. Since the vast majority of work in today's organizations is of a systems nature, it is unlikely that teams can operate in isolation. Hence, by the

leadership's encouraging—in fact, expecting—teams to collaborate together, the organization benefits from a multiple-team synergy not unlike the multiple-individual synergy that occurs within effective teams. In this final stage of reaching empowerment, the responsibility for looking broadly across the organization should be shifted from the senior leadership to the teams themselves as much as possible.

4. The self-directed teams should be called upon by the senior leadership to cross-train members within their teams in order to expand the overall team ability and to keep people on the teams excited by growing. The more everyone on each team can perform all the functions on the team, the better prepared the team will be. And one of the greatest rewards individual team members can receive in an empowered company is the opportunity to develop the use of new skills. An empowered organization depends on the growth of its people, and empowered people seek continued growth and development—a win-win situation for both the organization and individuals.

5. Empowered teams must continue to recognize and foster the value of the diversity of their team members. As has been promoted throughout the journey, the diversity of team member talents, knowledge, ability, and experience is a tremendous asset to an empowered team. By this stage of the process, the teams must be encouraged to fully realize the power of this diversity, while also achieving syn-

ergy of effort and growth. What this means is teams must continue to manage conflict and work hard to achieve synergy from the diverse opinions and styles of their members at any given point in time. It is through such synergy that the teams can achieve outstanding, even astounding, results. But these dynamics are not static. The teams must be encouraged to share their knowledge and experience with each other, thus reducing their range of diversity as people learn from each other. At the same time, the teams, through exposure to new problems and in concert with the different learning styles and experiences of their members, will develop new diversities that allow the cycle to begin again. Members of these teams will find that through their involvement in this process, they are rewarded in ways that far exceed any financial reward. Likewise, the organization will find that it has a process that continually renews the organization and aids in the retention of top quality team members.

How Do Teams Play the Role of Being Business Partners with Senior Management?

1. At this stage, the self-directed teams should have developed strong relationships with the senior leadership of the company. Information should be flowing smoothly between teams and leaders, as well as among the teams. In addition, there

should be a clarity of perspective flowing from an agreed-upon vision and set of values. With the teams functioning at a relatively high level of empowerment, what remains is the final cementing of a partnership between teams and senior leadership, as the teams replace the hierarchy with a relationship of effort and responsibility. The focus up to this point in the teams has been on operational improvements and innovation. Now the focus should expand to include strategic issues as well as business innovation. The empowered teams will have the information, perspective, and knowledge to offer suggestions regarding new strategic directions for the company. Which markets to enter, what products/services to offer, and other such strategic decisions must be considered jointly by the teams and the leadership if they are to be full partners. Likewise, changes in product design, new advertising campaign ideas, cost control innovations, and other such business innovation ideas must also be considered jointly by the leadership and the teams as they work in partnership. There can be no greater validation of the teams than for leaders to say, "We have a problem and would like you to help us solve it. Let's work on this together." While all teams may not yet be ready for this involvement, as they see other teams becoming involved as partners with leadership, they will have a clear idea of a goal for which to strive.

The senior leaders of a large equipment manufacturer that was faced with the prospect of downsizing also wanted to maintain their drive to empowerment. But how could they do both? Their decision was to share the dilemma with the teams and engage them in solving this problem. Rather than isolate themselves with this important decision that would affect profitability and morale, the senior leaders involved the entire organization—through the teams—in grappling with the decision. Many options were considered, including layoffs. In the end, however, the teams determined alternative ways to reduce costs that avoided the need for layoffs. Labor costs were reduced through attrition and job sharing, but the teams thought of a variety of ways to reduce other wasteful practices and their associated costs, as well as ways to enhance revenues. Resolving this problem not only saved significant amounts of money, it also solidified the partnership feeling between management and the teams, and it enhanced the culture of empowerment.

2. The teams should be asked how to make the culture of empowerment even better than it has become. By this stage of changing to empowerment, the original goals and scope of empowerment should be within range. Both leadership and the teams can now evaluate where to go next. The question to be discussed is, Just how far can

we take this empowerment concept in our organization? The scope of the self-directed teams can be reviewed to determine if there are more far-reaching decisions in which they should become involved. In addition, the information-sharing process can be examined to determine if additional information can be generated and shared that will help the company improve its performance. In both cases, the rich dialogue that is involved will enhance the feeling of ownership and partnership between leadership and the teams because it means that the teams are becoming not only operational partners with leadership but also strategic partners.

3. The self-directed teams should be encouraged to continue to raise the bar of performance standards in order to stay ahead of competitors in other companies. This means that continuous improvement efforts must be inspired because improvement efforts become more difficult over time. It also means that the teams and leadership must begin to seek out not just evolutionary improvements but quantum improvements, as well. Implicit in these statements is that the teams must join senior leadership in looking outside the organization for information about what competitors are doing, as well as for new ideas that range well beyond the industry in which the company operates. Environmental scanning both inside and outside the organization

must become the task of the teams working in conjunction with senior leadership, as both parties take on the responsibility of watching for both opportunities and threats to their organization.

4. The final element in the equation of partnership is to fully incorporate rewards, bonuses, profit sharing, and stock options (where possible) into the performance management system for the teams and their members. Of course, this means that leadership and the teams must share in the opportunity to benefit from improvements in the company's performance and in the risk associated with problems in company performance. The most promising way to achieve this level of direct responsibility is through stock plans and incentive schemes that allow for both positive and negative bonuses that are tied to company or site performance. The most progressive empowerment companies have pay plans that are comprised of an individual component, a team component, a site or department component, and a company component. And while there is a wide variety of means for achieving this combination, and a wide variety of weightings that can work, one common theme is reward and risk. When the company does well, all the partners (leadership, team leaders, and team members) benefit, and when the company does not do well, all the partners suffer together. The result is a very powerful

partnership based upon mutual interests and concerns.

CONCLUSION

We now have concluded our discussion of all three keys to empowerment—information sharing, creating autonomy through boundaries, and replacing the hierarchy with self-directed teams. You are ready to fully embrace the new culture of empowerment. All three stages of the change process—Starting and Orienting the Journey, Change and Discouragement, and Adopting and Refining Empowerment—have been navigated, and the organization and its members have been transformed into empowered people in empowered teams in a culture of empowerment. In the final chapter, we will summarize the journey we have taken and close with a challenge for your future efforts.

CONCLUSION

A LOOK BACK (AND FORWARD) AT THE JOURNEY

Wow! What a journey to empowerment. Looking back, the challenges have been great, but the resolve has been even greater. Eventually, everyone has pulled together to make the journey possible and to reach the destination of empowerment. As we look back through this book, we can now more fully understand just how involving and challenging it is to make the change from a hierarchical mind-set to a culture of empowerment, accountability, team pride, and job ownership. To leave the comfort zone of the hierarchy and move toward the unknown takes a vision, a faith in what it will mean to be empowered, and a continued effort over many months to finally arrive at a new comfort zone in the world of empowerment.

In looking back over the journey we have described in this book, we can also look forward to your journey. In this final section, we compile everything into an action plan for creating empowerment. Our hope is that this plan will provide you both perspective and inspiration to begin and/or keep moving on the journey to empowerment.

CHAPTER 12

Summarizing the Action Plan For Creating Empowerment

The journey to empowerment is one of the most challenging any set of people can undertake. It challenges and calls upon us to change many of our most basic assumptions about organizations. Furthermore, there is no one way to move from hierarchy to empowerment. Each company and its people will be different. Indeed, each manager and set of employees within a company will be different. What we have tried to provide in this book is a set of guidelines for navigating the journey. We have provided descriptions of many of the kinds of actions that will help in the change process. And in so doing, we have provided answers to many of the questions that leaders and team members have about moving to empowerment.

AN ACTION PLAN FOR THE JOURNEY TO EMPOWERMENT

To make the change takes real commitment and effort, but it also helps to have an action plan to guide the efforts of everyone involved. Indeed, it may be essential to a successful journey. It is critical to recognize that any organizational change will go through various stages if it is to be successful. As we have described in detail, the three stages of change are

1. Starting and Orienting the Journey
2. Change and Discouragement
3. Adopting and Refining Empowerment

Within each stage of the change process, different issues and concerns must be addressed, which means that the three keys will serve somewhat different functions and be played out in somewhat different ways in each stage of the change process. But it is critical to remember to use all three of the keys to empowerment throughout the change process, for without all three, some elements of the empowerment effort will fail and the entire empowerment process will be in jeopardy. The keys are dynamic, not static! Again, the three keys to empowerment are

1. Share Information with Everyone
2. Create Autonomy through Boundaries
3. Let Teams Become the Hierarchy

In creating a culture of empowerment, one of the major changes involves a movement from dependence on leadership from others to a condition of independence from, or interdependence with, leadership. To help guide this journey we used Situational Leadership® II and its application to four domains—self-leadership, one-on-one leadership, team leadership, and organizational leadership—together with the three keys to empowerment.

Let us try to summarize the overall empowerment action plan by overlaying the three keys to empowerment on the three stages of the change process in the matrix that follows. But before you turn the page, let us warn you that the list is quite extensive since it summarizes everything in this book.

We recommend that you consider where in the change process you are and then focus on the relevant parts of the matrix. For example, if you are just starting, focus on the first part of the matrix that deals with Starting and Orienting the Journey. Use the list of items under each key as a checklist of suggested actions to follow. Of course, feel free to add others that seem relevant to your situation, and do not forget to pay attention to the actions under all three keys. As you move forward and start to experience the Change and Discouragement stage, shift your focus to the actions in the second part of the matrix, again considering all three keys simultaneously. Finally, as empowerment comes into clear view, shift your focus to the actions in the third part of the matrix, the Adopting and Refining Empowerment stage. Again, remember to use all three empowerment keys.

One more comment before you turn the page: When you study the matrix, you may notice that some action items in the plan are similar, if not exactly the same, from stage to stage and even from key to key. Before you ask why, let us remind you, as noted in the first chapter, that the change to empowerment is hard work. Some areas need repeated focus if they are to change. And some questions that people have just do not go away easily. By judiciously using actions as needed, even if they have been used before, you are far more likely to reach the destination of empowerment. Tenacity drives consistency.

All right, now you can turn the page!

THE EMPOWERMENT ACTION PLAN

STAGE OF CHANGE #1: STARTING AND ORIENTING THE JOURNEY

THE 3 KEYS:

Share Information with Everyone	Create Autonomy through Boundaries	Let Teams Become the Hierarchy
1. Help people understand need for change	1. Recognize the hierarchy mind-set—boundaries limit action and responsibility	1. Understand that teams can do more than individuals
2. Avoid misinformation	2. Define boundaries to clarify what people can and must do	2. Begin to use team diversity
3. Explain how company makes money	3. Define desired responsibilities	3. Do not expect too much success early
4. Teach company financials	4. Clarify decisions employees will make and will not make	4. Teach team skills to managers and employees
5. Share some sensitive information	5. Explain company's business goals	5. Teach consensus decision making
6. Ask what information you would want as employee	6. Explain company vision and values	6. Teach team communication skills
7. List information people have and need	7. Set clear performance goals for people	7. Teach how to conduct team meetings

Share Information with Everyone	Create Autonomy through Boundaries	Let Teams Become the Hierarchy
8. Locate where information is now	8. Clarify priorities	8. Help teams see small successes
9. Start small	9. Teach employees business basics	9. Teach team members to hold each other accountable
10. Stretch but don't break your comfort zone	10. Teach managers to be coaches	10. Start early with teams using information
11. Share good and bad information	11. Teach decision making skills	11. Hold team information-sharing meetings
12. Use a variety of means to share information	12. Clarify small decisions people can make	12. Give teams small decisions to make
13. Share location- or site specific information	13. Teach problem solving skills	13. Begin to hold teams accountable
14. Share same information managers use		14. Share issues and involve teams in solutions
15. Use information to make people accountable		
16. View mistakes positively		

STAGE OF CHANGE #2: CHANGE AND DISCOURAGEMENT

THE 3 KEYS:

Share Information with Everyone	Create Autonomy through Boundaries	Let Teams Become the Hierarchy
1. Use information to align expectations with reality	1. Use collaborative goal setting	1. Have team leaders provide support and direction

Share Information with Everyone	Create Autonomy through Boundaries	Let Teams Become the Hierarchy
2. Share information to build pride in people's work	2. Discuss role of managers in relation to goal accomplishment	2. Encourage team leaders to expect more from teams
3. Encourage information sharing from employees up to management	3. Use team member ideas to set goals	3. Encourage teams to use their new skills
4. Train managers to listen better	4. Use a mix of team and individual goals	4. Be sure teams tackle challenging but solvable problems
5. Expect tough questions from employees	5. Get teams involved in determining problems for focus	5. Encourage team members to take leadership roles
6. Do not shy away from sensitive information	6. Focus on continuous improvement	6. Draw out team member ideas for improvement
7. Show people how their work has impact	7. Set skill goals as well as performance goals	7. Allow teams to tackle more complex decisions
8. Encourage team members to share information with each other	8. Begin to revamp the performance management system	8. Anticipate and work through stalls in team involvement
9. Praise improvements in performance	9. Build a performance partnership among team members	9. Continue to hold teams accountable for results
10. Praise teams that identify problems	10. Listen to concerns of people re performance management system	10. Allow team goals to drive performance
11. View mistakes as learning opportunities	11. Begin to devise pay system to treat employees like owners	11. Reduce department meetings; increase team meetings
12. Share information re change process and progress	12. Create a team-based performance management system	12. Anticipate team fear of failure; help teams stay focused

Share Information with Everyone	Create Autonomy through Boundaries	Let Teams Become the Hierarchy
13. Share even more sensitive information than in first stage	13. Broaden scope of decisions made by teams	13. Expect a lot from teams but not full synergy of effort yet
14. Use technology to efficiently share information	14. Move to creation of profit centers	14. Help teams see what they are accomplishing
15. Hold meetings with IT so it learns what information is needed where	15. Facilitate teams solving problems	
16. Show impact of small changes	16. Draw out ideas to change old policies and procedures	
17. Help teams see results of using new skills		
18. Create better links of rewards to performance		

STAGE OF CHANGE #3: ADOPTING AND REFINING EMPOWERMENT

THE 3 KEYS:

Share Information with Everyone	Create Autonomy through Boundaries	Let Teams Become the Hierarchy
1. Let teams determine what information is needed	1. Let teams take on expanded scope of decisions	1. Let teams use information and skills to play vital business role
2. Trust teams with information they request	2. Replace old hierarchical Boundaries with vision and values in people	2. Have teams begin to focus on strategic goals as their own accountability
3. Ask teams to inform senior management how they use information	3. Include team members in setting new boundaries	3. Encourage teams to integrate new team members

Share Information with Everyone	Create Autonomy through Boundaries	Let Teams Become the Hierarchy
4. Let teams work directly with IT to improve systems	4. Let team goals replace individual goals	4. Encourage teams to continue to work hard to stay a fine tuned unit
5. Stress that complete information sharing is vital to continuous building of responsibility and trust	5. Let teams monitor impact of their actions	5. Encourage teams to reach out to other teams re companywide empowerment
6. Let teams use information to hold themselves accountable	6. Let teams be free to set goals that relate to company strategic goals	6. Cross-train all team members for greater flexibility
7. Use information to indoctrinate new team members	7. Have teams use information to identify areas for improvement	7. Be sure that teams value and seek diversity of members
8. Continue to teach and reinforce values and expectations	8. Encourage team members and team leaders act as true partners	8. Have teams work with senior management on new strategic initiatives
9. Use information sharing to keep everyone knowledgeable of new changes	9. Use an ongoing performance management system built on team member and team leader partnership	9. Encourage teams to ask how to improve the company empowerment culture
10. Praise people who facilitate information sharing	10. Let teams make many of the old HR decisions	10. Let teams continue to raise performance standards
11. Continue to share information re mistakes so everyone can learn	11. Be sure teams and management stay on same measurement "page"	11. Have teams be fully included in benefits and risks of business partnership
	12. Let teams help create new business opportunities	
	13. Encourage teams to continue to seek operational improvements	

Share Information with Everyone	Create Autonomy through Boundaries	Let Teams Become the Hierarchy
	14. Reinforce team members as full partners in the business	
	15. Encourage teams to create goals that stretch management	

That is quite a list of actions to undertake. Fortunately, as noted earlier, not everything must be done at once. By dealing with each of the three stages of change as they occur, managers and employees on the journey to becoming empowered team leaders and team members can focus on a manageable set of issues. However, it is important to remember that all three keys must receive attention at each stage of the change process if you are to arrive at empowerment.

FINAL CHALLENGE

So, you may ask, what else is left for you, the reader. The answer is simple yet profound. Take this book and use it as a guide to creating an empowered culture in your company, department, or work unit. Do not focus on the difficulty of the challenge or on items you cannot change. Rather, trust the plan and the strength of your conviction to create empowerment. The destination is certainly worth the journey, and the journey will get easier more quickly when you have an action plan to guide you.

Why not be the best you can be and help others around you to be magnificent as well? That is what you want and what others want, too. On top of all that, empowerment is the right kind of leadership practice for company and personal success both today and into the future. We welcome you to the empowerment journey.

Notes

CHAPTER 1

[1]   See Edward E. Lawler III, Susan A. Mohrman, and Gerald E. Ledford, Jr., *Employee Involvement and Total Quality Management* (San Francisco: Jossey-Bass Publishers, 1992).

[2]   Ken Blanchard, John P. Carlos, and Alan Randolph, *Empowerment Takes More Than a Minute* (San Francisco: Berrett-Koehler Publishers, 1996).

[3]   For an interesting explanation of the model, see Ken Blanchard, Patricia Zigarmi, and Drea Zigarmi, *Leadership and the One Minute Manager* (New York: William Morrow and Company, Inc., 1985).

CHAPTER 2

[1]   See F. Hall and S. Hord, *Change in Schools: Facilitating the Process* (Albany, N.Y.: State University of New York, 1987).

[2]   Situational Leadership was originally developed in 1968 by Paul Hersey and Ken Blanchard. Significantly updated with the help of colleagues Don Carew, Eunice Parisi-Carew, Fred Finch, Laurie Hawkins, Drea Zigarmi, and Patricia Zigarmi, an explanation of Situational Leadership® II was published in 1985; see Ken Blanchard, Patricia Zigarmi, and Drea Zigarmi, *Leadership and*

300

the One Minute Manager (New York: William Morrow & Co., Inc. 1985).

[3]   See Ken Blanchard, Susan Fowler Woodring, and Laurie Hawkins, *Up Your Power: Situational Self Leadership at Work.* Escondido, Calif. (The Ken Blanchard Companies, 1998.)

[4]   See Ken Blanchard, Don Carew, and Eunice Parisi-Carew, *The One Minute Manager®Builds High Performing Teams* (New York: William Morrow & Co., Inc., 1990).

[5]   Contact The Ken Blanchard Companies, 125 State Place, Escondido, CA 92029 or call 1-800-728-8000 for information on *Situational Leadership®II and Change.*

CHAPTER 3

[1   Ken Blanchard and Sheldon Bowles, *Gung Ho!* (New York: William Morrow and Company, Inc., 1998).

CHAPTER 4

[1   James C. Collins and Jerry I. Porras, *Built to Last* (New York: Harper-Business, 1994).

[2   Kenneth Blanchard and Michael O'Connor, *Managing by Values* (San Francisco: Berrett-Koehler Publishers, 1997).

[3   Adapted from Jesse Stoner and Drea Zigarmi, *From Vision to Reality,* (Escondido, Calif.: Blanchard Training and Development, 1993), and Jesse Stoner and Drea Zigarmi, *Creating Your Organizations Future: Building a Shared*

Vision (Escondido, Calif.: Blanchard Training and Development, 1993).

[4 John P. Carlos, *Performance Planner Top 10* (Escondido, Calif.: Blanchard Training and Development, 1993).

[5 Trevor Keighley, *Self Direction Assessment (SDA)* (Sydney, Australia: Professional Training and Development, 1993).

CHAPTER 5

[1] Kenneth Blanchard, Donald Carew, and Eunice Parisi-Carew, *The One Minute Manager Builds High Performing Teams* (New York: William Morrow and Company, Inc., 1990), 21.

[2] Eunice Parisi-Carew and Don Carew, *Team Charter Leader's Guide* (Escondido, Calif.: Blanchard Training and Development, Inc., 1998).

CHAPTER 6

[1] Ken Blanchard, John P. Carlos, and Alan Randolph, *The Empowerment Barometer and Action Plan* (Escondido, Calif.: Blanchard Training and Development, 1995).

[2] Ken Blanchard and Sheldon Bowles, *Gung Ho!* (New York: William Morrow and Company, Inc., 1998).

[3] Kenneth Blanchard and Spencer Johnson, *The One Minute Manager* (New York: William Morrow and Company, 1982).

302

CHAPTER 7

[1] Kenneth Blanchard and Robert Lorber, *Putting the One Minute Manager to Work* (New York: William Morrow and Company, 1984).

[2] For more information on the training guide that has accompanied these efforts, see Alan Randolph, *Partnering for Performance* (Escondido, Calif.: Blanchard Training and Development, 1997).

[3] Trevor Keighley, *Self Direction Assessment (SDA)* (Sydney, Australia: Professional Training and Development. 1993).

CHAPTER 8

[1] Eunice Parisi-Carew and Don Carew, *Team Charter Leader's Guide* (Escondido, Calif.: Blanchard Training and Development, Inc., 1998).

[2] Trevor Keighley, *Empowering for Performance* (Sydney, Australia: PTD Development Trust, 1996).

CHAPTER 9

[1] Don Shula and Ken Blanchard, *Everyone's a Coach* (New York: Harper Business, and Grand Rapids, Mich.: Zondervan Publishing House, 1995).

[2] Ken Blanchard and Sheldon Bowles, *Raving Fans: A Revolutionary Approach to Customer Service* (New York: William Morrow and Company, 1993).

[3]   Ken Blanchard, Sheldon Bowles, William East-men, Barry Youngblood, Peter Psichogios, and Dev Ogle, *Raving Fans Gap Finder* (Escondido, Calif.: Blanchard Training and Development, 1996).

CHAPTER 10

[1]   Trevor Keighley, *Empowering for Performance* (Sydney, Australia: PTD Development Trust, 1996).

Acknowledgments

When you write a book to share what you have learned, you realize just how many people deserve praise and thanks. Over the years working with a wide variety of companies, teams, and leaders, we have learned many ideas and concepts that relate to releasing the power of people. But more importantly, we have grown to admire and respect the many people who engage in the empowerment journey every day of their lives and who help achieve astonishing results by releasing the power of people around them. Their efforts and inspiration have resulted in two books for us: the previously published *Empowerment Takes More Than a Minute* and the book you now hold in your hand, *The 3 Keys to Empowerment: Release the Power Within People for Astonishing Results.*

Let us start by recognizing the companies and the key contact individuals with whom we have worked and from whom we have learned so much:

1. All Pro Packaging—Bob Argabright
2. Allied Signal—Cindy Durnal
3. Americom Cellular—Mike Gill
4. Arrow Electronics—Kathy Bernhard, Grace Dervin, and Paul Nichols
5. Black & Decker Corporation—Dan Stiff
6. Cargill—Stephen Sebastian, Virginia Pimentel, and Jose Carabajal

7. Emerson Electric—Barb Tindall, Tom Dugosh, and Jeff Edgar
8. Environmental Elements—Ted Verdery, Jim Sinclair, Mike Dunseith, and Lisa Morris
9. Ethicon—Linda Morgan
10. E.I. DuPont Company—Mike Perry
11. Federal Communications Commission—Alan Schneider
12. Florida Power & Light—George Wilson (Jo-Anne Pitera and Barbara Dabney, formerly with FPL)
13. HCIA Inc.—George Pillari, Don Good, John Robison, and Susan Steele
14. Household International Corporation—Jeanne Gruner and the Performance Management Task Force
15. Howmet Corporation—Chuck Elledge and Karl Hamlin
16. Internal Revenue Service—Art Hylton and Liz Keating
17. Johnsonville Foods—Ralph Stayer
18. NewsWest—Shaun Conroy and Joel Shapiro
19. Pacific Gas & Electric Company—George Clifton (retired)
20. Pfizer—Cathy O'Connor
21. Price Waterhouse Coopers—Pat West and Jon Armstrong
22. Rocky Mountain Elk Foundation—Tracy Scott
23. Sartorius—Arnold Briesblatt
24. Stop & Shop—Bill Grize, Dick Baird, Gina Ventre, and SueO'Neil

25.   The Turner Corporation—Frank O'Connor
26.   Trader Joe's—John Shields

These companies and the people noted deserve much of the credit for what we have learned about the Three Keys to Empowerment and how they should be applied at each of the three stages of the change process. These individuals provided us with many of the questions you see in this book, and they helped us arrive at the answers. Indeed, they were our learning partners in navigating the empowerment process.

In addition, we want to thank a variety of people who have encouraged and inspired us to write the book in your hands. These people have also taught us much about empowerment at various stages of the journey. We extend our thanks to Jim Despain; Joe Viviano; Michael Cardone; Bill Pollard; Bob Buford; Ron Floto; Dennis Carter; Lewis Payne; Tom Jackson; Mike Squilante; Jeff Beck; Jim Waller; Irv Rule; Matthew Reimann; John Donnelly; Joe Bode; Bruce Dalgleish; Mike Louden; Joe Raymond; Lou Reymann; Rick and Esther Miller; Andee, Megan, and Madison Oleno; Kelly and Kaitlyn Antunes; Bob Cecil; and Ashley, Shannon, and Li Randolph.

Certainly, to this list we would add Steven Piersanti, our editor at Berrett-Koehler Publishers, who saw the need for a follow-up book to *Empowerment Takes More Than a Minute,* and encouraged us at every step in the process of completing *The 3 Keys to Empowerment.* We would also add to this list Pat

Anderson, Charles Decker, Kristen Frantz, Elizabeth Swenson, Maria Jesus Aguilo, Karla Swatek, Robin Donovan, Mike Vana, and many others on the Berrett-Koehler team for their hard work and support in bringing this book to you. And, then too, our agent, Margaret McBride, and her staff deserve a thank you for their efforts, as well.

We would also be remiss if we did not acknowledge the intellectual debt we owe to the many people whose colleagueship we value and whose work has been an inspiration to us. The list would clearly include our colleagues at The Ken Blanchard Companies, especially

1. Don Carew and Eunice Parisi-Carew, who taught us so much about developing teams;
2. Pat Zigarmi, Drea Zigarmi, Fred Finch, and Laurie Hawkins, who helped us see the expanded value of Situational Leadership® II;
3. Jesse Stoner, for teaching us about the power of visions;
4. Bill Eastman, Barry Youngblood, Pete Psichogios, and Dev Ogle, for teaching how companies can create Raving Fan customers;
5. Susan Fowler-Woodring and Laurie Hawkins, for helping us to understand how people can become Situational Self Leaders.

In addition, the list of people to whom we are intellectually indebted includes many of Ken's co-authors who are not a part of the immediate Ken

Blanchard Companies family but who are definitely part of the extended family. They include

1. Sheldon Bowles, who taught us the power of creating a Gung Ho! environment;
2. Spencer Johnson, who long ago taught us about the power of each minute that we have for influencing people;
3. Trevor Keighley of The PTD Group in Sydney, Australia, who taught us a great deal about the process of creating self-directed teams;
4. Michael O'Connor, who taught us the power of managing by values;
5. Bob Lorber, who shared the power of measuring and tracking performance as a power means for improving performance;
6. Paul Hersey, who taught us all about a powerful leadership model that came to be called Situational Leadership® II;
7. Don Shula, who inspired us by being a great leader as a coach in the National Football League.

The list of those to whom we owe an intellectual debt also includes many people whose work has inspired us to share our learnings about Empowerment, especially:

1. Peter Drucker, management guru to millions of managers;
2. Peter Block, author of *The Empowered Manager;*
3. Warren Bennis, author and practitioner of leadership;

4. Ed Lawler, researcher and writer on many organizational issues;

5. Steve Kerr, author and now practitioner at GE in the field of motivation;

6. Chris Argyris, Professor Emeritus at Harvard University and guru in the field of leadership;

7. John Kotter, Harvard University professor and acclaimed writer on leadership;

8. Jerry Porras, Stanford University professor and coauthor of *Built to Last;*

9. Noel Tichy, University of Michigan professor and writer in the field of leadership;

10. Robert Miles, Emory University professor and writer in the field of organizational change;

11. Barry Posner and Jim Kouzes, co-authors of *The Leadership Challenge;*

12. Jack Stack, president and CEO of Springfield Remanufacturing Company and author of *The Great Game of Business.*

About the Authors

Ken Blanchard is a prominent, gregarious, sought-after author, speaker, and business consultant. Few people have impacted the day-to-day management of people and companies more than Ken has. He is usually characterized by friends, colleagues, and clients alike as one of the most insightful, powerful, and compassionate men in business today.

Ken's impact as a writer is far reaching. His best-selling book *The One Minute Manager* ®, co-authored with Spencer Johnson, has sold more than 9 million copies worldwide and is still on many bestseller lists today. Ken has also had five other books in the last five years on the *Business Week* BestSeller List: *Raving Fans* and *Gung Ho!* (both with Sheldon Bowles), *Empowerment Takes More Than a Minute* (with John Carlos and Alan Randolph), *Everyone's A Coach* (with Don Shula), and *Mission Possible* (with Terri Waghorn). In addition, Ken has written several other books, including five more in the *One Minute Manager* ® library, plus Ken's own spiritual journey as documented in the book *We Are the Beloved.* Recently he completed his third book with Sheldon Bowles, *Big Bucks,* and a book titled *High Five* (with Sheldon Bowles, Don Carew, and Eunice Parisi-Carew).

Ken is Chief Spiritual Officer of The Ken Blanchard Companies, a full-service, global management training and consulting company that he and his wife, Dr.

Marjorie Blanchard, founded in 1979 in San Diego, California. He is also a visiting lecturer at his alma mater, Cornell University, where he is a trustee emeritus of the Board of Trustees.

Ken has received many honors including the prestigious International Management Counsels McFelley Award, putting him alongside such as honorees W. Edwards Deming and Peter Drucker. He also received lifetime achievement recognition from the American Society for Training and Development (ASTD), by winning the Distinguished Contributor to Human Resource Development Award. In 1992, Ken was also inducted into the HRD Hall of Fame by *Training Magazine.*

Ken and his wife, Margie, live in San Diego, California, along with their son, Scott, his wife, Chris, and their two sons, Curtis and Kyle. Their daughter, Debbie, and her husband, Humberto, also live in San Diego.

John P. Carlos is "an amazing storyteller!" His poignant, humorous, powerful, and practical storytelling style has been wowing audiences around the world since 1989.

John combines his business experience in the private and public sectors to create stories that are rich with the human condition and powerful with applications that affect his clients' personal and professional lives. John has the ability to draw people into his stories with humor and common sense. His talent for causing people to examine their own behavior first is a magnificent methodology for affecting change in organizations and personal lives. He has the ability to make people laugh while they learn.

John is a Senior Consulting Partner with The Ken Blanchard Companies, headquartered in Escondido, California.

In 1996, John co-authored his first book with Ken Blanchard and Alan Randolph, *Empowerment Takes More Than a Minute* (Berrett-Koehler Publishers, 1996). The book immediately climbed to number seven on the *Business Week* BestSeller List, and in less than four years has been translated into thirteen other languages. John is currently working on his next book, *Getting Hired by Your Team,* a collection of twenty-five best practices used by team leaders as identified by their team members.

John was voted one of the Outstanding Young Men in America and is a Vietnam era veteran of the U.S. Army. He is a member of ASTD, a member of the faculty of the American College of Physician Executives, and a graduate of the San Bernardino County Sheriff's Academy. He was awarded the "Key to the City" of Indio, California, for his outstanding service and is past president of the Running Springs Area Chamber of Commerce. He holds a bachelor's degree in business and a masters of business administration from Columbia Pacific University.

John and his wife, Lynne, live in Phoenix, Arizona. They have two grown daughters, Kelly and Andee, and two sons-in-law, Todd and Lino, plus three grandchildren, Megan, Madison, and Kaitlyn, all of whom live in Arizona.

Alan Randolph is well respected for his knowledge and insight into complex managerial issues. He is a sought-after speaker, consultant, trainer, and educator both domestically and internationally. Clients and colleagues appreciate Alan's ability to combine logic and a friendly humor into a style that makes complicated concepts and issues easy to understand.

Alan has worked with a wide variety of private and public sector organizations covering a wide range of industries, including small to large organizations, start-up, growing, and mature organizations. His specialties in speaking, consulting, and training include empowerment, performance management, project planning and management, leadership, and team building. Always clear and concise, Alan has an ability to connect with his audiences and to help them learn while having fun.

In addition to being a Consulting Partner with The Ken Blanchard Companies, Alan is a Professor of Management at the Merrick School of Business at the University of Baltimore.

He has published articles on a number of management topics in both practitioner and academic journals. He is coauthor with Ken Blanchard and John P. Carlos of the best-selling book *Empowerment Takes More Than a Minute* (Berrett-Koehler Publishers, 1996), co-author with Barry Posner of a popular book on project management, *Getting the Job Done: Managing*

Project Teams and Task Forces for Success (Prentice-Hall, 1991), and co-author with Robert Miles and Edward Kemery of the widely used organizational simulation *The Organization Game* (Addison-Wesley Longman, 1994). In 2000 Alan joined with Ken Blanchard, John Carlos, and Peter Grazier to publish *Power Up for Team Results,* a ten-booklet discussion series for teams to guide themselves to empowerment.

Alan's educational background includes an industrial engineering bachelor's degree from the Georgia Institute of Technology, plus a master's degree in personnel and industrial relations and a Ph.D. in business administration from the University of Massachusetts, Amherst.

Alan and his wife, Ruth Anne, who is also a Consulting Partner with The Ken Blanchard Companies, have three daughters, Ashley, Shannon, and Liza.

Your Stories and Questions

We want to hear your stories and questions about empowerment efforts in your organizations.

Tell us about your success stories (even partial successes deserve praise) and about your frustrations as you work to create an empowered organizational culture.

Do you know someone who deserves recognition for being an empowering leader or for being an out-standing empowered team member?

Do you have questions to which we can respond?

We are confident that you will have found this book useful, but we want to continue learning from your stories and questions. So please write to us at:

The Ken Blanchard Companies
1409 Locust Ave.
Baltimore, MD 21204
USA

And thanks for letting us hear from you!

Services Available

Ken Blanchard, John P. Carlos, and Alan Randolph speak to conventions and organizational meetings all over the world. Their messages are impactful and inspiring, as well as entertaining.

Additionally, The Ken Blanchard Companies, with whom all three work, is a full-service consulting company offering long-term consulting partnerships, seminars, books, workbooks, videotapes, and audiotapes in the areas of empowerment, team building, leadership, performance management, project management, and customer service.

For more information, please contact us at:

The Ken Blanchard Companies
125 State Place
Escondido, CA 92029
USA
Tel. 800-728-6000
Fax 760-489-8407
www.kenblanchard.com

The three authors may also be contacted directly as follows:

Ken Blanchard:
e-mail ken.blanchard@kenblanchard.com
or tel. 800-728-6000

John P. Carlos: e-mail mpowering@aol.com
or tel. 602-992-0320

Alan Randolph: e-mail randasso@ix.netcom.com
or tel. 410-321-8231

See Autonomy, creating through boundaries; Information sharing; Teams, developing,
people wanting to know how they will be impacted by, *113-114*
problems alleviated by, *6, 8*
reasons for changing to, *3-5*
reasons for difficulty achieving, *9, 11*
lack of understanding, *1*
stages in process of changing to, *14-17*
transition to, *30-31*
    feelings experienced in, *30-31*
Empowerment Takes More Than a Minute, *11, 13-14, 50, 59-60, 62, 82*
Everyone's a Coach, *230-231*

F
Failure, fear of, *227*
Fear,
  of failure, *227*
  of making mistakes, *82*
Financial ownership,

See Employee ownership opportunities,
Front line people, *67-68, 155, 157, 159*
information sharing and building responsibility in, *77-78, 80, 82, 168-169*
Frustration,
See Discouragement,

G
Goal setting, *104-105, 182, 184-186, 188, 259*
  collaborative, *261, 263*
  involving people in, *188*
  performance, *101, 103*
  performance improvement, *189-190*
  skill development and career enhancement, *192-193*
Goals,
  See also Priorities; Team goals,
  SMART, *101, 195*
  strategic, *260-261*
Gung Ho!, *80, 82, 160*

H
Habits, adopting new, *16*
Hawkins, Laurie, *37*

Situational Leadership II
Model, *11, 17-18, 20-21, 24-26, 50*
  applying to a self and
  team perspective, *35-36*
  development cycle, *33, 35,
  43, 45-46, 48*
  development levels and
  leadership styles, *26, 29, 45*
  goal, *25*
  is done with rather than
  to people, *37*
  lessons from, *90*
  matching leadership style
  to development level, *29-31*
  situational team
  leadership, *38-40, 42-43*
Situational Self Leadership,
36-38
Skill development, *192-193*
Skills, new,
  needed to operate in
  empowered culture, *105,
  107-110, 230*
  See also Team skills,
    learning business basics
    in the company, *108-109*
    middle managers'
    ability to explain
    reports, *110*
    problem analysis and
    decision making, *114*

related to information
  being received, *108*
SMART goals, *101, 195*
Stoner, Jesse, *97*
Structure, role of, *13-14*
  in traditional hierarchies,
  13
Supervising, over- versus
under-, *90, 92*
Systems changes,
  See under Performance
  management system,
  reducing departmental
  and staff meetings, *225*
  to support teams and
  hold them accountable,
  220-221, 223, 225

T
The One Minute Manager,
160-161, 170
Team accomplishments, *127,
129*
Team chartering process,
124
Team conflict, *271*
Team decision making,
138-139, 217
  with small decisions,
  135-136, 201
  stages of authority in, *219*

330

Books For ALL Kinds of Readers

At ReadHowYouWant we understand that one size does not fit all types of readers. Our innovative, patent pending technology allows us to design new formats to make reading easier and more enjoyable for you. This helps improve your speed of reading and your comprehension. Our EasyRead printed books have been optimized to improve word recognition, ease eye tracking by adjusting word and line spacing as well as minimizing hyphenation. Our EasyRead SuperLarge editions have been developed to make reading easier and more accessible for vision-impaired readers. We offer Braille and DAISY formats of our books and all popular E-Book formats.

We are continually introducing new formats based upon research and reader preferences. Visit our web-site to see all of our formats and learn how you can Personalize our books for yourself or as gifts. Sign up to Become A RHYW Registered Reader.

www.readhowyouwant.com

23305262R00190

Printed in Great Britain
by Amazon